AN ILLUSTRATED JOURNEY
INTO THE PSALMS

Landscape of Hope

HEATHER HOLDSWORTH

Moody Publishers

CHICAGO

Edited by Amanda Cleary Eastep
Interior and cover design: Erik M. Peterson
Cover and interior illustrations by Heather Holdsworth

Library of Congress Cataloging-in-Publication Data
Names: Holdsworth, Heather, author, illustrator.
Title: Landscape of hope : an illustrated journey into the Psalms / Heather Holdsworth.
Description: [Chicago] : [Moody Publishers], [2023] | Includes bibliographical references. | Summary: "Through the medium of art and words, artist and Bible teacher Heather Holdsworth shares an illustrated journey into the Psalms. Landscape of Hope takes passages that have become familiar-perhaps too familiar-and reveals their soul-strengthening, heart-restoring power"-- Provided by publisher.
Identifiers: LCCN 2023007182 (print) | LCCN 2023007183 (ebook) | ISBN 9780802429896 (hardcover) | ISBN 9780802473424 (ebook)
Subjects: LCSH: Bible. Psalms--Meditations.
Classification: LCC BS1430.4 .H65 2023 (print) | LCC BS1430.4 (ebook) | DDC 223/.206--dc23/eng/20230303
LC record available at https://lccn.loc.gov/2023007182
LC ebook record available at https://lccn.loc.gov/2023007183

Originally delivered by fleets of horse-drawn wagons, the affordable paperbacks from D. L. Moody's publishing house resourced the church and served everyday people. Now, after more than 125 years of publishing and ministry, Moody Publishers' mission remains the same—even if our delivery systems have changed a bit. For more information on other books (and resources) created from a biblical perspective, go to www.moodypublishers.com or write to:

Moody Publishers
820 N. LaSalle Boulevard
Chicago, IL 60610

1 3 5 7 9 10 8 6 4 2

Printed in China

For Adrian—
still can't believe I get to live life with you

Contents

Introduction

In the book of Psalms, there is beauty that lifts our souls from weary valleys to hilltop praise. Words flow across the pages like the swaying grasses of the lowlands; they climb the valley sides to become forests and rise on the updraft as soaring birds. These poems from a shepherd writing notes on a ridge carry us up to the heights. But he also writes of darkness that lurches into the landscape, that descends to hell's gates and cloaks communities with dread.

The Psalms are raw. They are bold. They peel off our well-formed layers, leaving us exposed. They invite us to explore the tensions of our souls—our hiddenness, failures, prayer-poverty, praise—they ask much of us. This sacred collection of poetry speaks *for* us, takes us to the essence of being human, moves us through seasons, and makes us more real.

The poet is not giving us a recipe for living—he *is* living.

Athanasius, fourth-century church father and philosopher, wrote of these poems:

I believe that a man can find nothing more glorious than these Psalms; for they embrace the whole life of man, the affections of his mind, and the motions of his soul. To praise and glorify God, he can select a psalm suited to every occasion, and thus will find that they were written for him.[1]

To help these writings enter into our days, the author adds notes above each work. He wants more for his ideas than for them to be wrapped up in parchment. King David brings breadth to his writing by placing it in an altogether different dimension: he turns his words into song. He gives instructions to choirmasters about which voices are needed, where to use sopranos or basses. There are nine musical instruments listed in the collection, adding their unique rhythm and tone. David moves his poetry from quiet lines on parchment into the breath and heart of a choir, into the fingers and lungs of musicians. His words that were once flat on a page now leap into chords and harmonies that fill the air!

As we come to the book you hold in your hands, you'll find David's poetry taken into another domain. Here the poems are interpreted visually. Their tone and drift is shown in shapes laid down in pen.

For more than a decade, I have filed drawings like these safely in binders on shelves. I've been hesitant to show them. It felt too personal to share these visual explorations with the Bible's scribes. The tension and unwashed faith they disclosed felt, if anything, confidential. A decade of requests from my husband, my sister, and a dear friend to open the binders and let the joy out finally wore me down! What you hold is a record of engagements with the author of Psalms and the Almighty.

It is perhaps unexpected to meet the Lord with a pencil and a sketchbook. For you, it may be hiking boots, a plectrum, or a bass. We can meet Him as He made us. What a freeing invitation.

Anselm of Canterbury puts such meetings into words . . .

> Come now, little man! Flee for a while from your tasks, hide yourself for a little space from the turmoil of your thoughts. Come, cast aside your burdensome cares, and put aside your laborious pursuits. For a little while give your time to God, and rest in him for a little while. Enter into the inner chamber of your mind, shut out all things save God and whatever may aid you in seeking God; and having barred the door of your chamber, seek him.[2]

I have been helped by the subjects we consider in these next few pages to better engage with the Psalms. The eight sections below will better prepare us to delve into the main text and images. They will move us beyond cherishing just the beautiful verses we put into frames to more, much more! We'll explore David's **friendship** with God and the ancient methods of **meditation**, **prayer**, and protesting grief (**lament**) that have strengthened this bond.

There's a section on **structure**, with fresh findings from scholars on the surprising and beautiful arrangements of these poems. We'll take time to consider the creative mediums of **poetry** and **art** and their part in the journey. There is also a brief personal account of the unexpected events that birthed this **illustrative approach** to the Bible and to God.

Entering into Friendship

When we hear of a friendship that's "uneven," where one party is powerful and the other is weak, there seems little chance it will succeed. If *we* are the lower one in the pecking order, we tend to choose smarter clothing for meeting our friend—the shirt without the wrinkles, the scarf without the rip. We feel the need to present ourselves in a favorable light and not divulge our shortcomings. And if conversation flows and they suggest we meet again, we mark that up as a win.

What is quite unmissable in the record of David's friendship with God is that there's no posturing or pretense. The shirt may be crumpled and the sandals scuffed, but that doesn't seem to concern either one. The dialogue is exposing, yet it's filled with rare trust; there's no anxiety in its tone. It's as if they've dispensed with the first decades of friendship and jumped right into those deep late-night talks.

> To be transformed by the psalms, one has to be willing to be engaged in a relational dialogue, phrase-by-phrase, image-by-image, stanza-by-stanza, book-by-book, and beyond … unlike literature merely telling us to "do this" or "do that," and thus placing a distance between us and the text, the psalms become a twirling dance anyone may join. The free-for-all invitation to participate.[3]

We are invited into that dance, brought into friendship. Is this our purpose; is this why we're here? What *is* "the chief end of man" that the Shorter Catechism asks us about? The astonishing idea comes in the liturgical reply: "Man's chief end is to glorify God and enjoy Him forever."[4] Surely the chief purpose of those who follow God is to do lots of good stuff—live sacrificially, be the most generous, excel on mission, and surrender their lives.

The surprising welcome of the Psalms is to live carefree in God's bliss,[5] to have fun delighting in the Eternal! And what's more, this relationship is reciprocal—God delights in us. Oh, let's get a head start on "forever" and live untroubled, enjoying Him now!

The glory of God is a human being who is fully alive.[6]

Meditation

There is joy to be found in the Bible, in meeting its characters, in pondering its wisdom. But our approach to the text and to connecting with God can become dull. Obscured by comparison and guilt, busyness and pain, the relationship with God that began with vitality can lose its bloom. We may try to fix it with activity and shiny projects, but that conflicts with the invitation of Christ to His followers:

> "Are you tired? Worn out? Burned out on religion? Come to me. Get away with me and you'll recover your life. I'll show you how to take a real rest. Walk with me and work with me—watch how I do it. Learn the unforced rhythms of grace. I won't lay anything heavy or ill-fitting on you. Keep company with me and you'll learn to live freely and lightly." (Matthew 11:28–29 MSG)

Contentment in a life with God isn't achieved by bustle. It is slower; it is birthed over time by pondering His thoughts, allowing God to finish His sentences. Praise and thanksgiving, requests and lament—all of these emerge from a contemplation of God, from pausing with Him in our days.

Selah.

At times, these pauses are planned, giving us space to think. At times, they arrive uninvited. They daze us.

It was 2009, during the disorienting days of losing my mum and my dad, when I found that the words from the Bible I studied each morning wouldn't stay in my head. It's my practice to read and speak to God in prayer, but in the numbness, nothing stayed inside. At a time when I needed the solace of God, the words that normally brought strength flew away.

My brother told us that you see more animals on a safari when you go 10 mph rather than 30. The animals are all there, but the faster speed doesn't allow your eyes to settle, and you miss out on the wonder of it all.

We are not made for rushing. In the slower lane of these artistic ponderings, the discoveries have filled me with wonder and hope.

The years ticked on, and for my husband, Adrian, and I, life after my parents' passing became fuller. We changed country, jobs, homes, and community. Then right in the middle of my purposeful living, the world arrived at the pandemic of March 2020. I became gravely unwell with Covid-19, and the illness decided to stay. During days and months of extraordinary weakness, I turned to the psalms of lament. Restricted to the couch for nearly a year, with a small fold-out table to draw on, I opened to King David's

dialogue with his powerful Friend. It was profound and moving. As I sat each day drawing and meditating on his words, my fears were stilled by the peace of God and the room was crammed with bliss.

Slow reading and creative meditation have been the steadying joy in both these seasons of disorientation.

Prayer

We could be forgiven for thinking that for faith to be done "right," it needs excitement and proclamations. Our ordinary days seem a bit unexciting; they lack banners of triumph and euphoric praise. We may think that for faith to *really* work, it needs shiny people who are more "put together."

So, we concentrate on service, on what we can do. We make meals for the sick or drive Sunday school kids to camp—measurable things that allow us to feel like we've still got some skin in the game. But inside we retreat to silent spaces because faith that seems to work for the people on the stage clearly doesn't work for us. The friendship we once enjoyed with God feels beyond our reach.

In the early 1800s, Danish theologian Søren Kierkegaard spoke of those who found themselves in this place. He said that they were becoming a "gentle Christian,"[7] resigning themselves to a life without the living waters of Christ.

We can grow up to be tidy, more acceptable, less real. Our messy prayers are hidden in journals in the attic along with old toys and broken things. We didn't get it right.

But we did.

> If you want a boring prayer life, practice being good in it.[8]

From the earliest story where the Creator walks with Adam, to the wide-open exchanges David has with Jehovah, the people of God have prayed. Prayer is built into every dimension of Jewish living, it's not simply for festivals and sacred events. From the kitchen to the bathroom, from daybreak till darkness falls, each location, time, and emotion are lived with the Author of life. Prayers are recorded for all situations.

> I give thanks unto You, Adonai, that, in mercy, You have restored my soul within me. Endless is Your compassion; great is Your faithfulness. I thank You, Adonai, for the rest You have given me through the night and for the breath that renews my body and spirit.[9]

God is interested in our ordinary routines—there's something reorienting in that. The Alpha and Omega being attentive when we pick up kids, meet with a manager, deliver groceries to a neighbor, install a sink. There's no delay until we're presentable and no need to wait until Sunday. The conversation happens right where we are. It is earthy and honest and real.

There, in the stuff of our everyday living, we bump right into God. And we finally realize He isn't looking for show.

> We can nowhere evade, the presence of God. The world is crowded with Him. He walks everywhere incognito.[10]

Lament

To my amazement, as I started to draw the first fourteen psalms, I found eleven laments. *David, did you plan to drown us in gloom, to cover your readers with your questions and doubts? Surely you should lead with conviction, with steady belief and show us how to meet with God.*

I hadn't noticed his lamenting before because I was looking for the good bits, for verses I could underline and write on notes above my desk. But David takes us along alleys, past groups of men ensnared in vice. There's danger in the darkness that makes us want to run. But in the middle of distress, while we're looking for exits, he stumbles right into hope. David finds courage and faith in the anxiety of

the small hours, before anyone has turned on a light. And it is glorious.

It makes us think that this could be our story. And as we read on through the Bible books, we're given more hints that it could be true.

God's arrival into our world was without ritual and style. Born to an unwed teenager in a farm shed, He began His life under the shadow of shame. Hounded from birth by those resenting His power, He was no stranger to pressure. Friends who were close, walked away; some mocked, others fawned. He lived the full array of human emotions till that Easter week, alone in the darkness, He faced His end. God in the dust, God as dust. He has been where we live, where we wander and walk; He knows who we are. He never asked us to impress Him, to meet Him with pretense. David's songs of lament make that clear. Over seventy of the one hundred and fifty songs are shaped this way, with the poet calling to God, explaining his problem, making requests, recalling the past, and moving, despite danger, toward trust. He gives us the shape of hope.

> The Psalms are a reality check to keep prayer from becoming sentimental, superficial, or detached from the real world.[11]

David charts an untidy relationship with the Almighty that, were we to jump to the comforting "hug verses," would ring pretty false. He studies four themes: God, the wicked, the righteous, and himself. He asks questions, makes observations, and meets each subject head-on; his frustrations aren't pushed underground. There is room to shout, to tremble, to ask questions, to stay real. It's a path of mess, yes, and a path of hope. For if God works in this space, then He works!

He *has* lead with conviction, with steady belief. He *has* shown us how to meet with God.

Structure

Having thought about processing real life through poems, the book of Psalms might feel like a jumble. It is cluttered with authors from King David to songsters to the sons of a rebel priest. It doesn't stick to one theme but sings songs of praise then switches to lament and protest; there are lyrics of trust in difficult times and then bursts of exuberant thanksgiving. It seems to lack a linear movement or a clear narrative journey.

We may think our task, if we're giving a talk or leading a meeting at church, is to smooth the rough edges of this confusing work; choose a few of the highlights and tidier parts that will bring order and peace to the gathering. For the Psalms can beautifully enhance church programs and punctuate learning with spiritual depth. Shouldn't we find where the poet moves from angst to praise, and read out the bits where he's fixed, so we can feel better too?

But is the purpose of the songbook to decorate our worship and tie our faith up with a bow?

Much inspiring research over recent years has taken a long look at the Psalms and has found that there is strikingly more.

When a wonderful book is recommended to us, we arrive at its pages with expectations. There'll be a beginning to intrigue, a middle to surprise, and an ending to impress! Beginning, middle, end—this is what we've known since C followed B, since 4 followed 3, since we were seven.

When we open a Bible book it's no different. We expect Genesis to flow from Eden to Egypt, and for Judges and Kings to move us through time. In the stories of Jesus, Matthew, Mark, and Luke start with His birth and end with resurrection, water to wine; and good Samaritans are found in the middles.

But when we open the Psalms, our expectations are different. We tend not to ask too much of them. We could be forgiven for thinking that serious theologians would not choose this material for their life of study. For centuries it's been the go-to place for those who are wounded, not for those on the up-and-up. There's a slight feeling that the authors aren't coping too well; at times David doesn't seem all that stable. When we're looking for theology, we go to Paul for legal argument; and for accurate history, Dr.

Luke is the one. These are reliable people to build our faith on, their arguments are easy to follow. With the Psalms, well, it's different.

But what if there is more? What if the Psalms have a shape and a plot, with edited movement and a rising storyline. What if the editorial team committed to say something through the positioning of each poem? What if Psalm 8 follows 3–7 and 14 follows 9–13 so that we grasp something subtle and brilliant? What if the charting of friendship between a dust creature and his Maker is profound, not only in content but in where each entry is placed?

What if this book was put together with more intricate intention than The Lord of the Rings? Just as we don't hear of Sauron before Frodo leaves the Shire, or of the importance of the quest until he embarks on the journey? What if the book of Psalms has movement, plot, blossoming revelation, intention, and heat? What if it is more than a convenient spot to offload emotion?

If the Psalms are more than a music storeroom, where (if you're lucky) the scores have been returned to the right shelves … if it's a place to find theology, to grow faith, to see God—well, that changes things.

It changes everything! The Psalms are filled with intention. This book is not organized in chronological order, for the young shepherd-nobody defeating Goliath is placed after

David has been crowned king; and the death of his infant son in the palace comes when the monarch is in exile, far from his home. The timeline is all jumbled up. No, it's not in order of years; it isn't meant to be. The editor is doing something extraordinary: he weaves artistry, symmetry, and absolute wonder into this remarkable collection.

You may wonder what prompted my choice of fourteen psalms—Why have such an obscure number for a book? A dozen seems more pleasing, or, as this is written in Europe, perhaps keep things metric and choose a multiple of ten! Below you will find the reason: the outline of the first fourteen chapters of the book of Psalms. And while insight and wisdom permeate the poems, the symmetry adds layers of beauty. Here we see hints that the Psalms are curated, a collection put together with care and intent.

Significant Arrangement of the Psalter[12]

Instruction in the Godly Life under the Reign of God

BOOK I : PSALMS 1–41

Ps 1–2 Introduction, framed by two **ashre** ('Blessed is/are') declarations

1 Evokes instructions of Torah [Law] and Hokmah [Wisdom]

2 Evokes Former and Latter Prophets (Yahweh and his anointed, Israel's only hope in the turmoil of history)

Thus

1. *The Psalter must be read in the context of the rest of the OT canon.*
2. *As portal to the temple of the Psalter, these two psalms teach that those who would appropriate the prayers and praises of the Psalter must fit the profile of the framing declarations; their lives must be shaped by Law and godly Wisdom, and they must "take refuge" in Yahweh and his anointed—the two components of "the fear of Yahweh."*

Ps 3–14

64 lines

3 Plea for deliverance from foes

4 Plea for relief in time of drought

5 Plea for deliverance from foes

6 Plea for healing

7 Plea for deliverance from foes

8 Praise of the Creator (the glory of God bestowed on humans)

64 lines

9 Plea for deliverance from hostile nations

10 Plea for deliverance from the wicked

11 Trust in Yahweh's righteous rule

12 Plea for help in an ungodly time

13 Plea for deliverance from serious illness and enemies

14 The folly of humankind ("The LORD looks down . . . to see . . . all have turned aside")

The foundation stones are laid with Psalms 1 and 2. They speak of wisdom and royalty, of blessing and prayer. There are parallel movements to Psalms 8 and 14 with a symmetry of lines in the Hebrew text.

From Psalms 3 to 8, there is movement toward Zion and the longed-for presence of God: the psalmist first sees a holy hill on the horizon, a distant temple, and then, with dignity and exuberant praise, he arrives in the courts of God.

Then in Psalms 9 to 14, we chart his withdrawal as descriptions of evil intensify and the situation grows ever bleaker. We end up far from Zion where the arrogant rule and humanity is disgraced.

We aren't told who organized the songs in this way, who decided what went where. But what we see in this grouping from 3–14 is a need for proximity, an ache to be close to God. This flow is embedded in the text.

The Psalter isn't intended as a database of quotes to augment our worship and decorate our days; it has far more to say.

Art

Adrian and I had been in the city of Chicago for a couple of months when we set out to meet some new friends. The GPS said it'd take five minutes less if we took its suggested route. We walked halfway down the street, too far to turn back, when we heard the shouts of rage. Teenagers flew out of the house to our left, expelled by the tempers behind them. They vented loud frustration on yesterday's beer cans, and kicked their way down the street. I glanced up at Adrian. We were silent, eyes wide. This wasn't the shortcut we expected. He squeezed my hand to look ahead. Just past the fences and burned out apartments, young men on the curb began to move into a circle. Power and vice congealed around them; their shoulders were up, hoods shadowed their eyes. Goodness, we should have turned right.

Our eyes searched the block ahead to assess its danger as we picked up our pace. And there it was. We came upon it by accident. At the heart of the landscape, inside of the gloom, was a startling piece of art. Shredded cloth and plastic bags were intricately woven into a chain link fence. The font was beautiful but the word—the word took our breath away.

It read, "Hope."

There was stillness in this spot that changed the climate all around. We forgot our race for safety; we were quiet, stood closer. The artist had reached through the untamed space, and pressed faith right into our souls. In a place that pulsed with shame and fear, he wasn't running anger management classes or offering quick fixes in shiny binders. The word announced we were not at the end, we were only in the middle of the story!

For thousands of years, artists, craftsmen, musicians, and poets have lifted their tools to translate what they see. With cloth or with quills or with sable brushes, they painted glorious last suppers, fear-filled apostles; they told dark tales of shipwreck and dying messiahs. Craftsmen fused colored glass to let the sun shine the Bible in puddles of light on cathedral floors.

We stand before all these depictions, astounded. They have taken us far beyond what we can see and helped us to grasp what is holy. They've read the accounts and sat with the stories, interpreting tone, painting anxiety and faith.

The images in this book were born out of pondering the words and phrases of fourteen psalms. During the enforced rest on my "Covid-couch," I mulled over the biblical text. For hours each day, the more I saw, the more the lines took on shape. I've been astonished at the riches in David's words, the treasures he found in the darkness.

Art gifts us time. It is unhurried.

Poetry

Poems allow big ideas to land in deep places in us. They let us tremble at exposed emotion, tug at threads of sorrow and let things unravel. For poems, especially the Psalms, speak not only to us, but for us.[13]

Poems let us ponder; they are slow. They can feel indulgent!

Here is the tension: we're busy people, wired to achieve and get a great deal of things done. Poems ask a lot of us. We have to ponder questions, step into our fears—honestly, who has the time? The words feel disordered and a little unruly. They don't spell out a message of what we should do. Their plots are untidy and often unresolved. *Come to us with answers and a chart, and then we can plan. Spare us from the middle of the story!*

On Sundays, when we come to church, we assume we'll learn more about God; that the pastor will quarry each biblical text to bring us clear information. We assume logical patterns and clever directives will arrive at our pew, packaged and neat, and that by the end of the service he'll have fracked the passage for fuel that will power our days.

But in our eagerness to put things in order, we sometimes forget to hear what God says. Words are not given to master; ideas are not there to consume. The poetry of the Psalms is for wonder, for mystery, for engagement with the Eternal on cardinal things.

When policies need to be outlined, when important things need to be said, we in the twenty-first century use arguments and prose. Our legal documents are not in verse or accompanied by a lute! There are no biblical tears in bottles, no trees clapping their hands, and no soaring on eagles' wings![14]

But in ancient times, the vital things in life were recorded in verse. One-third of the Bible is poetry recorded in the Hebrew form, where lines repeat and intensify, where thoughts develop in pairs. The last words of poems don't sound the same—the cat doesn't sit on the mat by the rat—that's not how these poems work. It's the *ideas* that rhyme, not the sounds. It makes for a deeper contemplation.

Poems invite pondering. They take the calendar of life, where meetings are scheduled and reminders ping, and move us to the heart level, where all the action is. The Psalms add tone and movement to factual accounts:

- We can read about David's throne being seized; 2 Samuel records it. But the tension in that story between a king and his son, we enter into in Psalm 3.

- The story of the giant warrior Goliath and the terrified armies across the plain is written in the book of Samuel, but the marvel of the win is in Psalm 9.

- David's taking of Bathsheba and murder of her husband is chronicled in cold detail in the book of Kings. But we hear the ache and the prayer in Psalm 51.

- And the crucifixion of Christ—the trials, the timings—are charted meticulously in the New Testament. But to discover the depth of the darkness He entered and to hear the prayer He prayed, we need Psalm 22.

Poems fill in the gaps; they give us more.

The psalmist is giving us his journal without gluing any pages together—things that lie unanswered are rough and fought through. He's written it all without gilding over the losses or ignoring the joys. This isn't some record of prim religiosity—these are songs between friends in the middle of the story. That is where they were written, and that is where we live.

In these pages, David is known; it is safe; he belongs.

A Helpful Approach

Landscape of Hope takes the writings of the psalmist and gives a visual description of what is taking place. It takes time over the meaning. Art describes; it rarely dictates. These images are an invitation to slow down.

Paired with each picture are comments of application, of how the psalmist's ideas work out in life. These are not intended as an analysis of the Hebrew language or a commentary on theological debate. These remarks are written for slow reading. There is room to reflect and to ponder with a cadence in the words that is not for speed, but rather for contemplation. There may be details in the Bible commentary that seem unfamiliar—there are one of two reasons for this. It could be the use of a little creative license based on what we are told in the text. Or, more likely, it comes from details that are given elsewhere in the canon. I've spent the best part of three decades teaching young people what is found in the Bible. I find joy in searching through obscure Old Testament passages in Judges or Chronicles, Amos or Kings, to see who was alive when, which characters interacted, and what was going on in their kingdoms. Color, surprise, and nuance are brought to stories that are often hastily told. Each illustration depicts a portion from a psalm with words written out (perhaps multiple times) to show the movement of David's thinking.

To "read" the image, find the beginning of the verse with your eyes, or even better, with your fingers. The phrases may be tiny or swirling around, but travel with the sentence, sense the action and meaning, the shrinking and growing through the words of the song.

And ponder.

A Picture of Faithfulness—
A Song of Wisdom

The waiting congregation rises to sing as the keyboard begins an earnest tune. A hymn of trust, joy, and surrender beams at us from the screen to carry us into the program.

I'm not ready. My heart is still thumping from the fist-shaking man outside, upset when I stupidly pulled into a no parking zone. The morning news was appalling . . . the brutality of that gang, and little Emma Green is still missing. And on the way into church, I bumped into someone I was meant to meet up with last week. Trust, joy, surrender? I come feeling flustered, guilty, and unwashed, with last week's grime still glued to my soul.

Come stand by my side . . . let my heart settle . . . take me slowly to God. Walk with me softly; let me find beauty and mystery. Allow me time to understand there is something more . . . there is someone far greater than us. For if you feed me a script and speed me to an altar, the ritual will float over my life and leave me untouched, removed.

Psalms 1 and 2 are the doorway to the Psalter, the welcome that ushers us into these poems. At this threshold, there is time. Time to remember who we are and what things are about. It's a meditation in the presence of our divine Friend.

Later, we'll walk through this door and settle into its rooms, and speak of struggles and failures, oppression and strife. And we'll meet the characters, themes, and questions of the Psalms that are introduced in these first eighteen verses.

But first, we stand in this liminal space.

We're told the Psalms are "a teaching manual for worship and prayer"[1] and "for spirituality, for relationship with God."[2] If this collection is all about prayer, you'd expect that to be where it starts. But Psalm 1 is not about speaking with God—it's the wisdom song to show us where praying begins.

We have a tendency to run for the answers, to tune in to sound-bites, find the key 1, 2, 3s. We're busy people with networks to maintain, media to update, and information to pass on in ten seconds or less.

But God is in no hurry. In Psalm 1, He shows us how we can meet; and it's the same way He met people in the early Bible stories.

When the Israelites walked from the clay ovens of Egypt, there were weeks of hiking along arid tracks. Their whip wounds and memories mixed with freedom and hope as they followed Moses, the old shepherd, once prince. They rounded a bend, and their horizon filled with Sinai, the Mountain of God.[3] And then came lightning and sulfur and terror and trumpets and explosions and trembling and smoke! These days would hold God's epic revelation of a new society where virtue would trump power; where a higher law would stand over governments and kings: the Ten Commandments would change the world.

As we're gripped by the story in Exodus 19, the action pulls us in; we brace for the meeting between Moses and the Almighty and the writing on tablets of stone. But something takes place before the encounter, before Moses sets off on his climb up the hill. We read that a gift is given to the people who gathered, and that gift is the gift of time.

The slaves were not dragged to the mountain to make hasty commitments; this was no power ambush. The meeting with God would be three days away, and each person was to be dressed in clothes that were clean.

Three million tunics in the desert of Sinai sank into basins of water. Bloodstains and dirt from building sites in Rameses released their hold on the linen and poured away. And all around the encampment, floating on guy ropes between family canvases and hanging from poles, the washing blew, like a sea of white surrender in the wilderness heat.

At dawn on the third day, little ones and teenagers, mums and dads, all came washed to the mountain. They waited there. The astonishing sea-splitting, locust-growing, frog-forming, death-defying, darkness-making God gave them space to think, to wait, to take off the grime and make themselves ready.

Psalm 1 doesn't race up the hill to get the key information, doesn't give hasty solutions we can quickly apply. Yes, it holds structural beauty, symmetry, artistry, and a great deal of poetic punch; yes, it's put together with intention and its themes weave through the Psalter to end in bursts of praise. But it is far more than this. Its claims reach into us to show us the path to flourish in our humanity. Psalm 1 shows the route to deep satisfaction, and the ways that joy can be lost.

It maps the things that diminish a life, that break it down to chaff. It speaks of the places we take our bodies, the people we choose as friends. It studies the disintegration of kindness and how we use our minds. We may expect Psalm 1's advice to a life that is shrinking would be to simply reverse the choices we make: get advice from good people, hang out with the virtuous, make sure we do things that are kind.

We can be brilliant at evaluating our goodness—a few behavior modifications and we're right on track! But that is not the opposite of the life that falls apart. This poem is far more constructive than that. The counsel that's given is not to hide among others; it's to marinate in the wisdom of the Word of God. To savor it, relish it, be nourished by its beauty, and be taken into the bliss of God.

Psalm 1 is overflowing with grace; there is beauty, the righteous are blessed. The God we imagine to be irritated with our patchy prayer life or excuse for devotion sees us, not through frustration, but with generous love. We can stop studying our feet and look into His face. His welcome invites us to joy.

Undeserved kindness changes things.

There were two Liams in Miss Craven's class. One wrote extra sentences, helped those who were weaker, tidied his station, and was a delight. The other Liam was a nightmare. He was. If he made it to class on time, he ducked about in the line, pulling girls' hair or throwing rocks at their bags. Come lunchtime, there was fighting over shoes, over lies, over football, over anything. It never stopped.

With the first parent-teacher meetings scheduled for that night, Miss Craven collected the pile of misdemeanors. She had much to say to the second Liam's folks. The other Liam's workbooks were bursting with stars, and smiled up at her from a neat pile in the tray.

A weary mum, with a toddler on her hip, slumped into the chair in front of the teacher. With a deep sigh she mumbled the name of her son. Miss Craven was ready, pulling over the books, her face lighting up as she spoke of the boy. The mum's head shook in wonder. She brushed a tear from her cheek; things were at last looking up. She hugged her Liam at the gym hall door, relaying his teacher's gushing praise. Miss Craven looked up, to see her scamp of a pupil studying his mum's flushed, happy face.

The teacher reeled at her mistake, but the next parents were waiting, and she didn't have time to fix the slip. The following morning she wasn't sure what to do, when a young boy, shirt pressed, hair combed, face shining, stood waiting at the front of the line. He'd smoothed his workbook flatter and had painstakingly finished each of his homework sentences. Stunned at the change, she smiled toward his desk. He made his way over, and looking up, whispered, "I never knowed, Miss. I never knowed you thought I was all right." Liam thrived that year. And the next, and the one after. His teacher's accidental approval changed the path of his life!

In the stunning poetry of Psalm 1, we see a human being flourishing, taken up into the life of his Creator. The joy causes him to meditate more, the meditation causes more pleasure. There is purpose and strength, growth and a future. The image pulsates with acceptance.

Psalm 1 finds us looking up, whispering for joy, "We never knowed, Master. We never knowed You thought we were all right!"

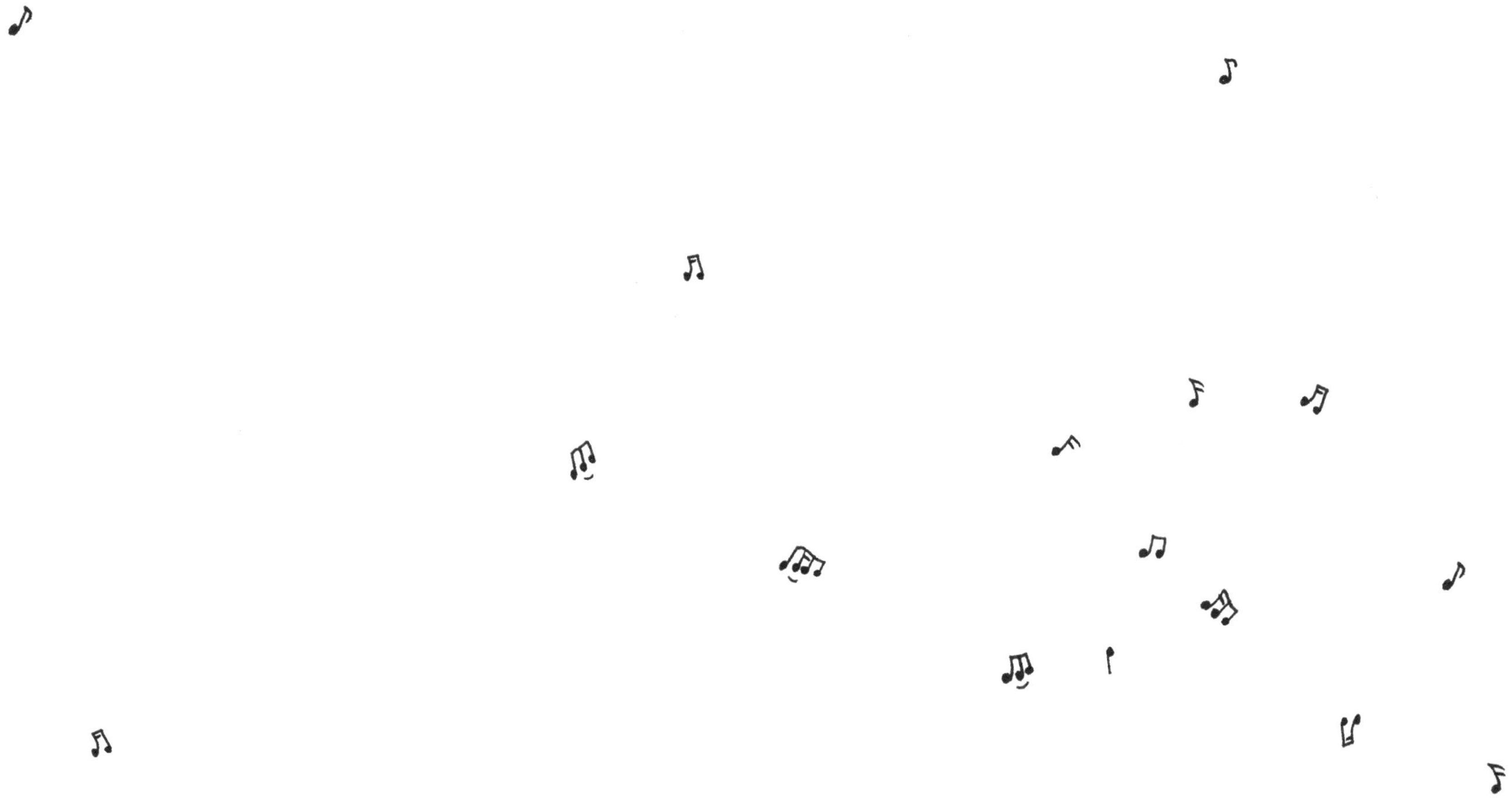

Pull up a chair

Blessed is the man
Who walks not in the counsel of the ungodly,
Nor stands in the path of sinners,
Nor sits in the seat of the scornful;
But his delight is in the law of the LORD,
And in His law he meditates day and night.

PSALM 1, VERSES 1 AND 2

The opening psalm in this three-thousand-year-old collection is the preface to the whole book of Psalms. It's the trailer that offers a sneak peek at the adventure without giving too much away! The psalmist has chosen the setting, the characters, and the tensions that lie between them. He introduces four concepts that will develop throughout the next 149 poems: God, the wicked, the righteous, and himself. We watch as he unrolls the blueprint for the entire Psalter, and he does it with a story of contrasts …

We are introduced to a pathway, shadowed by scorn, darkened by conceit. To travel it is to keep in step with those whose lives are vain. Companions on this road are slow moving; they are comfortable standing aloof. They easily pull up chairs to jeer at those who look weak.

And we wonder: What is the result of a life that sits down with these advisers as friends?

We're invited to consider an alternative route that is startling in its contrast. The atmosphere along this way shimmers with delight. The Guide on this path speaks to us through a text that values peace over popularity, humility over pride. Its wisdom pours stability into his frame. It gives purpose to his days and, rather than scrutinizing others, lets him see their needs. His mind comes alive. He discovers deep rooted contentment—"blessing."

The conclusion to this song reverberates through the Psalter—sitting around belittling those who aren't us, that's absurd. Today, let's turn to the psalmist's source of joy, and live the life we've been gifted.

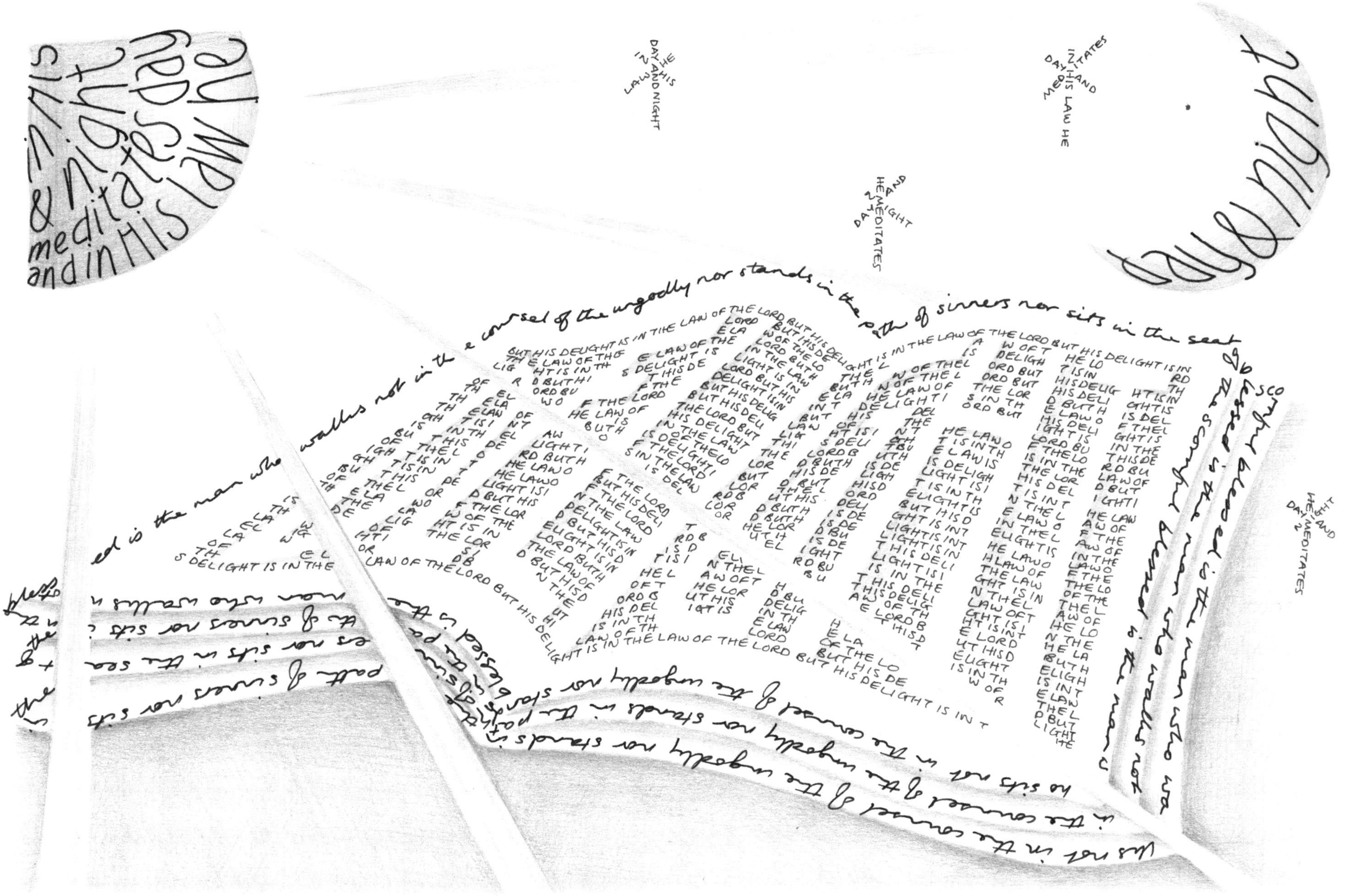

day & night meditates and in His law
day and night
blessed is the man who walks not in the counsel of the ungodly nor stands in the path of sinners nor sits in the seat
BUT HIS DELIGHT IS IN THE LAW OF THE LORD

What we're made for

He shall be like a tree
Planted by the rivers of water,
That brings forth its fruit in its season,
Whose leaf also shall not wither;
And whatever he does shall prosper.

PSALM 1, VERSE 3

There was a year I drew trees: giant redwoods, gnarled oaks, palms, magnolias. I think I drew every tree in Edinburgh's botanic garden! Even going to get groceries, I'd stop the car by an oak, pull a sketchbook from my bag and trace out the majesty. What captivated me? It was the strength of their trunks. They weren't going anywhere. Rain or shine, they stood calm. Unfazed. I was drawn to their solidity at a time when there was little.

There are a handful of trees in the biblical writings, and the description in verse 3 is one of the most beautiful. It pulsates with energy, does what it's made for; it flourishes! The solidity of it draws us in—the seasons, the river, the fruit, the green.

The strength it describes comes from a choice not to stop growing; not to spend days mocking those who pass by (verse 1). The health comes from long meditation on wisdom that works, on values that honor—we can drink deeply of that life-giving stream. It's where we will grow; he sings, and where we'll find peace.

On this riverbank, we become what we're made for.

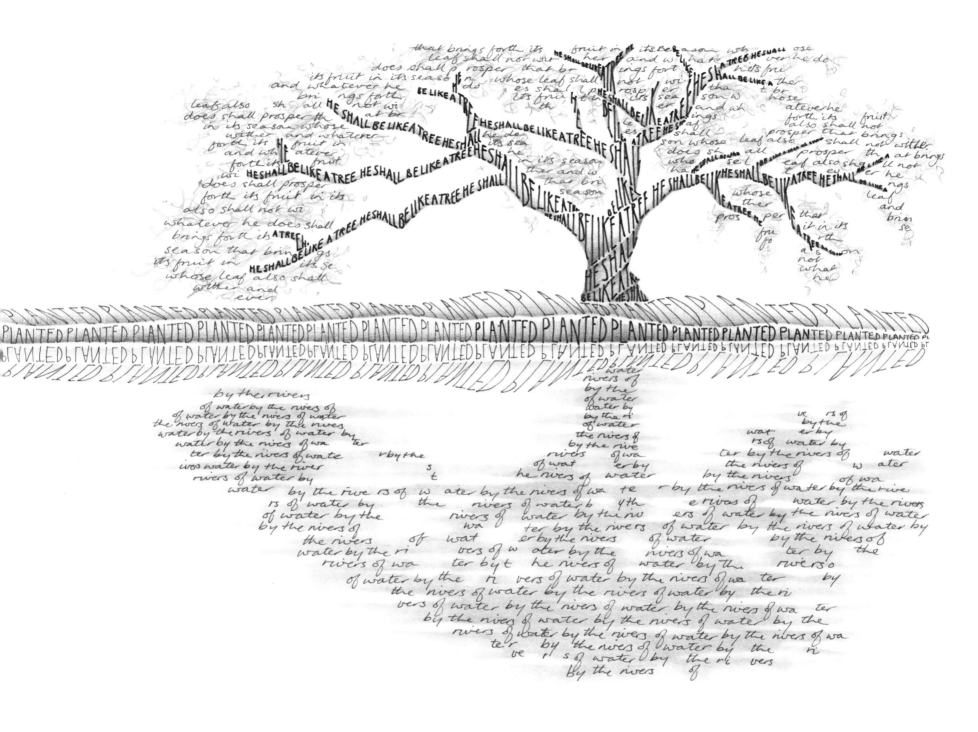

Weight watcher

The ungodly are not so,
But are like the chaff which the wind drives away.
Therefore the ungodly shall not stand in the judgment,
Nor sinners in the congregation of the righteous.

PSALM 1, VERSES 4 AND 5

When we think of an apocalyptic judgment day, an image of people being blown away by the wind is not what comes to mind. We imagine trumpets and terror and fire and storm; at least that's how the movie makers portray it! But the ancient songwriter crafts a different image.

We're at the end of time and all the peoples of the earth are gathered on an endless plain, trembling, waiting, listening. They look largely the same standing side by side, still. How can they be tested, evaluated, known? How will they be distinguished, one from the other?

He writes that the judgment of our souls comes not by fire and trumpets, but by a sifting wind. He draws on a rural picture, a harvest.

All the days of each plant are wrapped inside their seed. The kernel holds promise and consequence. It is filled with life, with plans for a future—this is how the psalmist identifies "the righteous." They are energized by God, giving their whole being weight.

The chaff is dry casing. It is blown from the grain because there's no substance to it. It is hollow. There are no roots to spread and no tree to grow. Nothing connects it to the future, and so, holding no life, the husks and shells disperse on the wind. Discarded.

This seems a more chilling judgment than the movie drama.

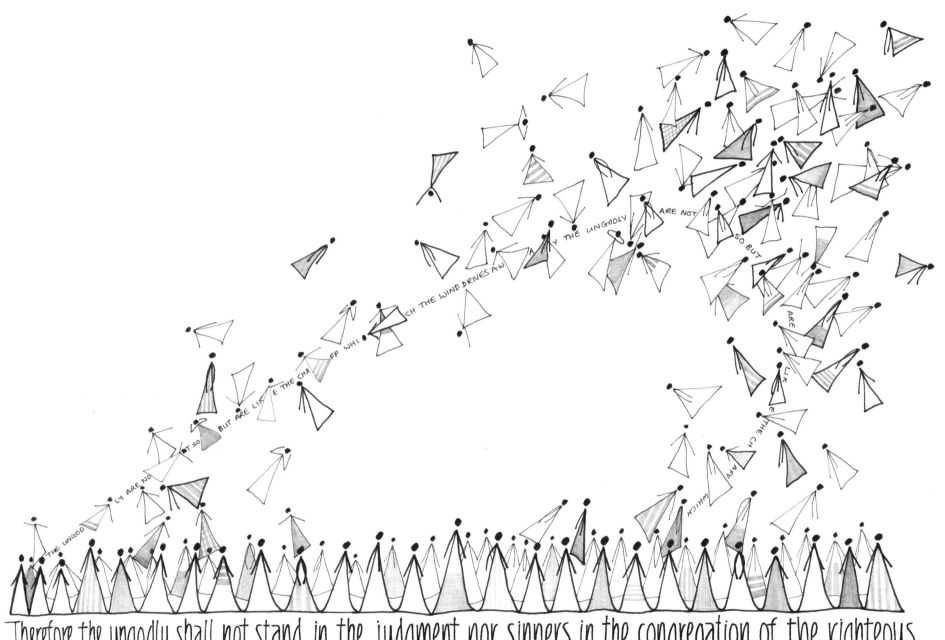

Therefore the ungodly shall not stand in the judgment nor sinners in the congregation of the righteous.

Outfoxing God

For the LORD knows the way of the righteous,
But the way of the ungodly shall perish.

PSALM 1, VERSE 6

As the days and years pass in the life of each person, character is revealed. With each step through time, integrity and vice are exposed in the community. Here we stand, this song declares, a result of decisions made and ambitions followed. Nineteenth-century philosopher-poet Ralph Waldo Emerson captured it well: "The force of character is cumulative. All the foregone days of virtue work their health into this."[4]

Every movement made is recorded through time, clearly seen by the eternal Onlooker. There's no hiding or projecting of a canonized self! We are seen; we are known.

The path of the righteous, states the psalmist, is in an eternal connection, a living bond. The way of the wicked, their desires and dreams, are cut off from this union, this life.

The contrasts in this song pull us to the tree by the river (verse 3), refreshed, rooted, and fruitful. They invite us to make choices on this day, in this hour, to strengthen those roots.

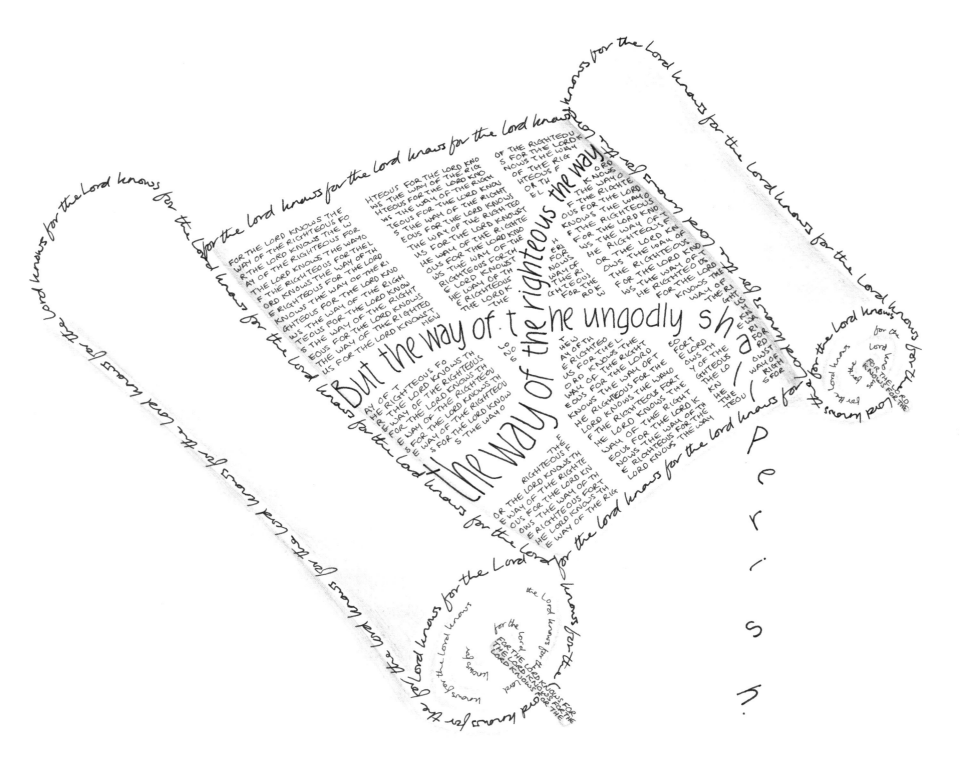

But the way of the ungodly shall
the way of the righteous the way

Perish.

The Kingdom of the Son— A Royal Song

Psalm 2 is not the ballad you'd play to walk down the aisle or to celebrate your Nan's ninetieth birthday. It begins with anger, leads with questions about rage. There's no reflection on goodness, on beauty or praise. We find King David perplexed.

He has known only friendship, wisdom, and justice from God; what makes the nations so irate at His rule?

The song maps out the extent of God's reach, the scope of His command. It is difficult to overstate how big the lyrics about God are in this passage of Scripture. The song is monumental, it towers above. In the 1600s, Stephen Charnock attempted to describe His majesty. It warrants a slow consideration:

> Imagine One who is excellent without any flaw. A Spirit who is measureless in size, priceless in value, who is present at every point of space, who is matchless in power, limitless in understanding, perfect in wisdom, who is light without darkness and infinitely more beautiful than any creature, who is purer than light and brighter than the splendour of the sun. And when you have risen to the highest, see him as infinitely above all you can conceive with the fullness of your thoughts. And whatever concept comes into your minds, say, "This is not God. God is more than this."[1]

The joy comes in that final phrase—we attempt to do God justice with our theological imaginings, then step back feeling silly that we thought we were getting close! How magnificent.

The next part of the psalm is a surprise. The eternal God speaks of an anointed One who is separate from Him, yet equal to Him . . . One who is adored, who stands in power, and on whom He pours eternal honor. God's Son is invited to approach His Father and make an enormous request. To ask, not for a house or castle, a region or country, but for "the nations." For *all* of them—He asks for everything that is! And His request is met with an unhesitating, "Yes." It is all His, plus "the ends of the earth."

But why ask? If the intention is that they're going to be His anyway, why go through the exchange? Why not simply give?

Psalms 1 and 2 are preparing to take us into a journey of prayer. It is the essence of the Psalter. To show us that when nations rage, when people oppress, when trials fly into our face, when failure torments, when we ache for forgiveness, the posture we take is to ask.

Charles Spurgeon, the nineteenth-century preacher, wrote, "Whether we like it or not, asking is the rule of the kingdom."[2]

So the Son approaches His Father to show us the way to share in the life of God. He helps us to see that a child of the King, however strong or uncertain, can come before Him and ask. It is the most glorious exchange a human can have, to be given a place before God.

It was my first time leading the afternoon Christian Club at the school in our town. I'd taken on the role from our much-loved leader, Peter. He was raw, adventurous, filled with faith—he believed stuff. One afternoon when his family were over for lunch, I passed the dining room where he sat with his young son. I held my breath as I heard him thanking God for carrot sticks: "Let these carrots make Josiah strong like a tree growing on a riverbank, putting down roots and being full of Your Spirit." Wow, it was real.

So, I was a little intimidated that first day as the fifty or so children filed into the gym hall. I glanced up at the two wonderful retired club leaders. We needed to bring things to order. "Let's all sit on the benches. Yes, that's it. Great to see you at club today. We're going to start with a prayer."

Have you ever used prayer to bring silence? We can use it to fill space, call people to order, or just because it is expected. I absolutely wanted the Lord's help; it's what I prayed for as I prepped. But, truth be told, my eyes were on the program, not the presence of the King of glory.

If I was looking for prayer to call for order, the announcement had the opposite effect. The children stopped talking, yes, but just as I closed my eyes, I heard a scuffle. Three of the older children turned their backs to me. What was this? I watched, transfixed as they knelt, elbows resting on the benches. Half a dozen stepped out and hunched themselves small on the floor, hands out, waiting, expecting the Almighty to hear. One moved from the row and went to the back, lying prostrate, face down . . . oh, and another was doing the same at the side. I was dumbfounded. With the "Amen" came whispered requests of "Can I pray, Miss?

Can I? Can I?" The room tingled with expectation.

They brought Him their granny's illness, their dad's job loss, their temper, their neighbor's suicide. All arrived unfiltered, expectant. God was massive and was listening and was reigning over all—you could feel it. I opened my eyes and saw hands shoot up, to get a chance to tell how prayers were answered last week.

As the children filed out, I turned to the two leaders, shaking my head in astonishment. Their eyes twinkled, "Oh, yes, Peter just finished a series on prayer."

The honor, the trembling, the expectation—they shook me that day. These young people showed up at a club that was mocked as the nerdiest in school, and they engaged their minds, hearts, and bodies in unreserved worship. They gladly chose to be under God's rule.

Psalms 1 and 2 begin and end with the conditional blessing of God: live before the Almighty, relish His wisdom, and you will find deep delight. Trust His royal rule, speak with Him through your days, and you'll be at rest in the life of God.

Stones in our shoes

Why do the nations rage,
And the people plot a vain thing?
The kings of the earth set themselves,
And the rulers take counsel together,
Against the LORD and against His Anointed, saying,
"Let us break Their bonds in pieces
And cast away Their cords from us."

PSALM 2, VERSES 1 TO 3

There is a belief that to follow God well, we need a life of restriction with stones in our shoes, that the proof of devotion is pain. Please, no!

Through his years of friendship with the Almighty, hardship is not what the poet has felt. He's puzzled that rulers are raging at God, for he's found refuge in trusting One who is stronger and found the wisdom he needed to lead people well.

Yet, in the palaces around him, those who rule over nations seem to balk at there being someone greater than them. Perhaps fear of a King they're unable to conquer—is that what allies them in seething and scorn?

Interestingly, when reporting the trial of Christ in the first century, Luke makes a strong connection. He sees the Jewish king Herod ally with Rome and condemn Jesus for political gain. He remembers the ancient alliance made by kings against God in Psalm 2, and labels "the Anointed" One as Christ (Acts 4:25–26).

In this poem, we are told there are two ways to be. The first is to give homage to the Infinite God; and the second, to join with others and ridicule His strength.

King David is baffled by the massive mistake, for connection with God is the best chance kings have of living a life that's fulfilled. Why do they rage when the cost of bowing to the Mighty is small?

Shoving castles

He who sits in the heavens shall laugh;
The Lord shall hold them in derision.
Then He shall speak to them in His wrath,
And distress them in His deep displeasure:
"Yet I have set My King
On My holy hill of Zion."

PSALM 2, VERSES 4 TO 6

Here we encounter power and weakness, God and the nations—the two are ludicrously mismatched. At all of their raging, the Almighty chuckles (I tried to draw a big trinitarian belly laugh, with guffaws pulsing across the heavens)!

We can understand the chuckle. To witness such an outburst would be, for us, like watching a two-year-old throw a tantrum after stubbing her toe on a castle wall. With fury she hits at the fortress, trying to push it out of her way. The walls stand unmoved, twenty-feet thick, while the toddler screams her disgust.

It's absurd. Go inside and enjoy its shelter; don't waste your strength in such folly!

We are told that the petulant anger of the nations grows a "deep displeasure" in the heart of God. For their contempt is based on a distortion of Him; their fury is built on a lie. The Alpha and Omega, the Transcendent Creator, rises at their rage. (I must confess I expected lightning bolts, and hints of Armageddon!) But His words speak of a plan to *help* them, despite their offensive disdain. His Anointed, His Son, will come to bring them relief.

This cuts into our caricatures of God where we imagine Him obsessed by our every infraction. He meets their scorn with kindness. What a baffling beauty.

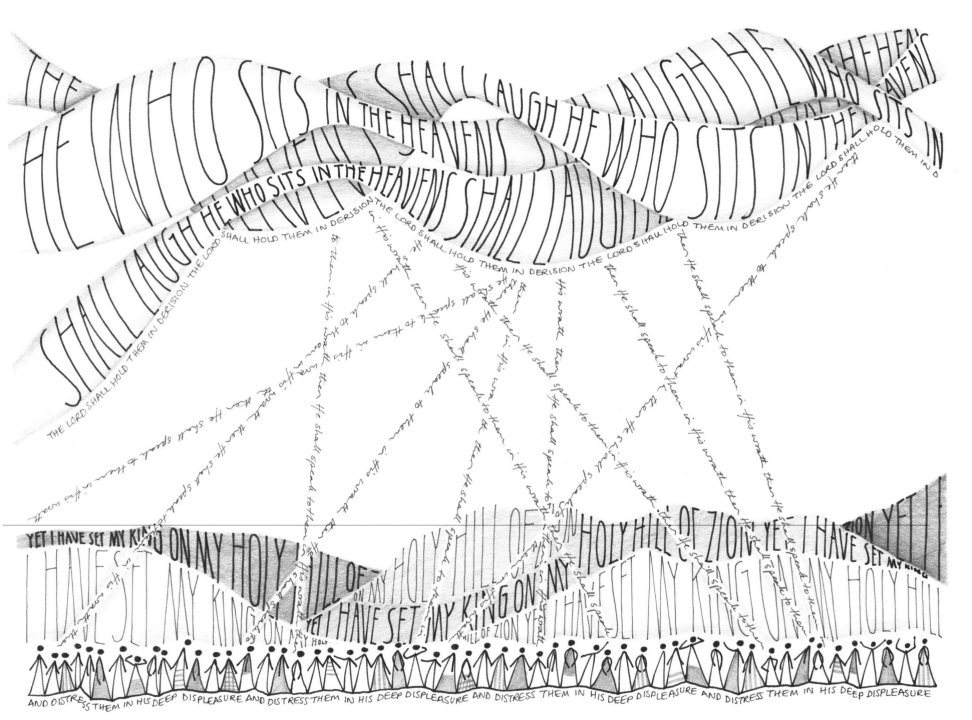

Sweet and sour

"I will declare the decree:
The LORD has said to Me,
'You are My Son,
Today I have begotten You.
Ask of Me, and I will give You
The nations for Your inheritance,
And the ends of the earth for Your possession.'"

PSALM 2, VERSES 7 AND 8

This is one of those spine-tingling messianic passages where "the Anointed" gives a blow-by-blow account of what is happening in the eternal realm.

I imagine it being read with a fanfare of trumpets, as huge statements rumble over the landscape. It is capped by a magnificent bequest that is universe wide and creation deep.

But did you spot the choice of word that would trigger all the bounty?

"Inheritance." David, surely this is a slip of the tongue. Don't you mean gift? For I remember inheritance. The devastation. The wreckage. The loss. The treasures of my parents became ours to hold, but the cost . . .

Is this three-thousand-year-old text hinting at some future sorrow? The possession of nations at the price of Himself?

I found myself trembling at those four syllables: inheritance. There's only one way to get that.

Choices, choices

"'You shall break them with a rod of iron;
You shall dash them to pieces like a potter's vessel.'"
Now therefore, be wise, O kings;
Be instructed, you judges of the earth.

PSALM 2, VERSES 9 AND 10

I've been learning a lot about trust, as respiratory illness does a dance in my lungs. For all our clever ways, our abilities don't extend to being able to breathe out and breathe in. We have little control over the smallest of things. But we do have choices. Hour by hour, thought by thought. We have an option to lean in to truth, to the source of it; to trust in the integrity of the One who holds sway.

The poet maps out for us where power lies and the character of the One who wields it.

The verse is alarming: there is breaking and dashing and shattering here. The writer says that people, despite their limitations, can stand in defiance against the Eternal, can shake their fist in His face, and scream of their lot . . . but there is an alternate way. In the middle of phrases of startling force, there's an unexpected invitation:

In the light of what's coming, and the power on display, O kings, make a choice—and let it be wise! God gives them a chance to trust in His leadership, to submit themselves to His power.

Now therefore be wise O kings; be instructed you judges of the earth

Royal chambers

Serve the LORD with fear,
And rejoice with trembling.
Kiss the Son, lest He be angry,
And you perish in the way,
When His wrath is kindled but a little.
Blessed are all those who put their trust in Him.

PSALM 2, VERSES 11 AND 12

How do you serve with joy, fear, and trembling? Surely, joy is the word that needs to be kicked out of the group! Serve, fear, tremble—that cluster makes more sense; it nods to oppression, even enslavement.

But David has written the word *joy*. And its presence changes the tone.

I wonder.

That we clean our homes is mundane and necessary. But if I were asked to clean rooms in Balmoral Castle, the royal family's Scottish residence, I'm not sure I could contain myself; the delight may overwhelm! Is that where the text is going, an honor so great it takes all your effort not to burst into applause?

Then come the words "Kiss the Son." That's uncomfortable. What is it doing in the prelude? If this signals the theme for the songbook, I must confess, I'm uneasy. But a little research shows that to kiss a leader in those days was not inappropriate intimacy but homage. The kiss was on the feet, not the face!

It's menial stuff, dusting rooms, cleaning feet. Yet, we're left in wonder and trembling joy. Everything changes because of who it's for.

Fleeing from His Son Absalom— A Lament of David

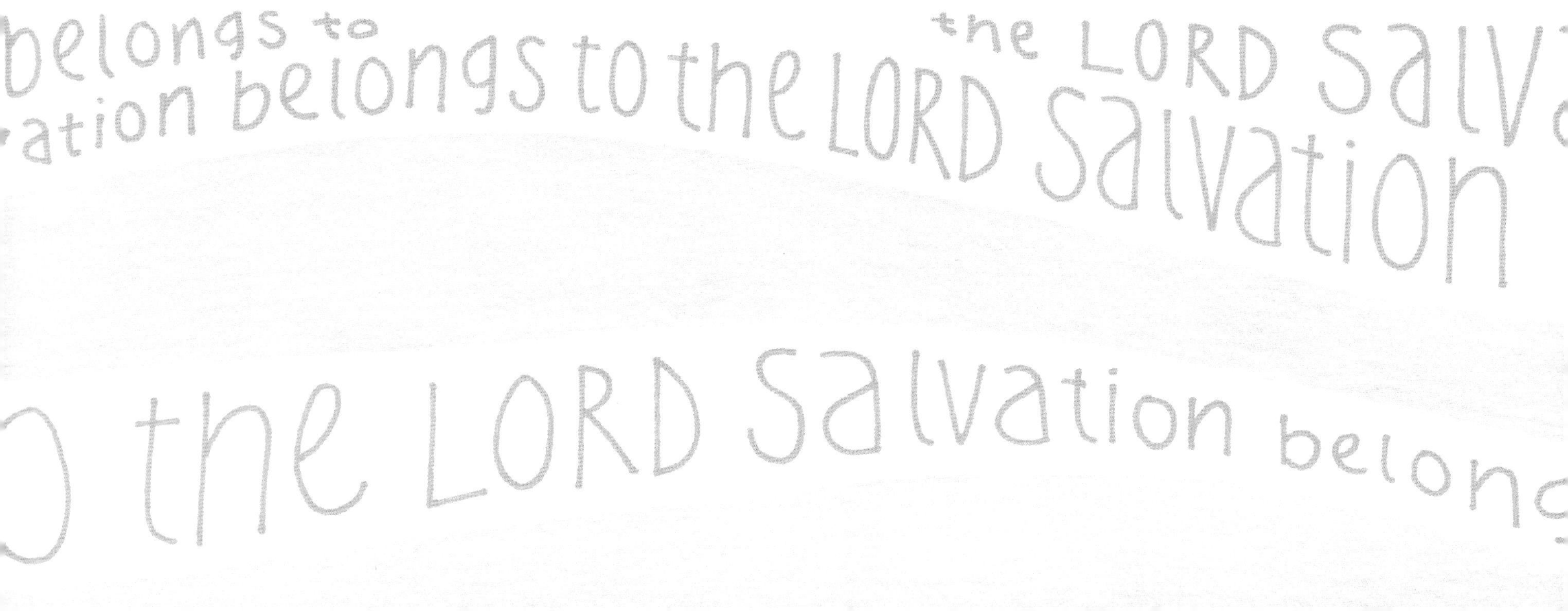

belongs to
ation belongs to the LORD
the LORD Salv
salvation

the LORD Salvation belon

It's the wrong way round. Children hide from parents when they've broken the vase, drawn on the wall, stayed out too late. Unless it's a game, parents don't run from their kids. Whatever happened for David's son to chase him from his home, to hunt him down like an animal?

Could the title be a typo, or added later by mistake? No. The heading is real. Someone thought it important to tell us what was going on.

In the history of Psalm 3 lie all the big crimes, the ones that rip at your soul. Is it the evil committed against Bathsheba (2 Samuel 11:27) and the murder of her spouse? In a way, the wrongs behind this lament are far more destructive. For they begin in the place where we're meant to feel safe; where things should be solid, where your dad has your back. They begin with relationships that hold people together, that give us identity. The mess of this poem takes place in David's family. Family. We ache when things go wrong and rest when all is right.

This tale may be the most marring in all David's story.

David's family was complex; it took "blended" to new levels. The position of king in those days came with expectations—power, authority, and a slew of wives. David did not disappoint. To his wife Ahinoam, his first son was born. Prince Amnon made David a dad; this little boy running round the throne room was heir to the kingdom. To David's wife Maacah, a son and daughter were born: Prince Absalom and then Princess Tamar.

You could spot King David's daughters all around the citadel. Each princess wore an exquisite robe, its colors announcing her lineage (2 Samuel 13:18).

The attack on Tamar was planned. She was helpless. Amnon feigned illness and asked her for food. He trapped her, defiled her, and after the fury, he had his servant hurl her like waste onto the street.

It was her brother Absalom who found her, cloak ripped apart, colors flying from unraveled seams. Her face and hands were smudged with ash; her body still shook with the violence. Absalom gathered his beautiful sister into his home and absorbed the horror.

The crime, like an erasing wind, removed Tamar from view. Her life collapsed within her, and, the text tells us, she "remained desolate in her brother Absalom's house."[1]

David found out. David did nothing. He did nothing for hours. He did nothing for days. He did nothing for months. He did nothing for years. He made no move to stand up for his little girl.

While Tamar became a shadow in Absalom's home, Amnon strode as successor around the countryside. It was too much. The silence and injustice twisted Absalom's soul. He made a plan to avenge his sweet sister and sent servants to end Amnon's carefree life.

After three years of exile for killing the heir, Absalom returned. He received judicial pardon from the palace but no audience with his father. But he needed forgiveness, not a legal pass. He asked for weeks. He asked for months. He asked for years.

He asked to speak to the man who had raped Bathsheba, who'd killed her spouse, who'd been pardoned for it all. He begged forgiveness from David who, in deep sorrow, had been shown mercy. And he heard nothing.

It was now seven years since Tamar's desolation. If letters weren't reaching the palace, maybe smoke signals would. Absalom set fire to the field of David's right-hand man. With the dousing of embers, an audience was granted.

But the damage was done; the rejection had wounded Absalom all through. This forced forgiveness brought no relief. So the prince took those who were closest to David, who held the place he so craved. He befriended the king's companions and won their loyalties.

He then weaponized his resentment and hounded David out. David ran for his life, trading Persian rugs for rocks, palace fare for dusty insects. But the anguish around those desert fires was not at the loss of his opulent world; his pain was far more profound.

I wonder if the worst family pain rises when we played a part—we withheld forgiveness and she died while she lived; we pushed him away, and he couldn't stop falling. That pain opens a wasteland in us, a vast emptiness where a question throbs: "If I *had* shown kindness, would we be here?"

Psalm 3 has been penned by a grubby hero. A complex character who, by his inaction, rained loss on his family and fractured his home. He's no flawless protagonist; he's a tangle of history, regret, mess, and hope. And as he leans hard on his God, David finds courage to get up and walk again.

He speaks to us; he speaks for us. We allow others to see our success but often inhabit wild spaces inside where dreams died, where plans were shot to pieces. There's mess and there's joy, grubbiness and regret.

And the hope to get up again.

Shields up

LORD, how they have increased who trouble me!
Many are they who rise up against me.
Many are they who say of me,
"There is no help for him in God."
Selah
But You, O LORD, are a shield for me,
My glory and the One who lifts up my head.

PSALM 3, VERSES 1 TO 3

We build spaces for peace, apartments and palaces, adorning the walls with our memories and joy. And to enter the safety, we each turn a key, a small, flat token that tells us we're home.

Into the stillness of King David's palace comes uproar and alarm. His door has been breached; a throng has pressed through. And who is the tyrant that's leading the fray? There's appalling recognition of the one at its head. Fury has erupted from the boy he ignored . . . from Absalom. This war has been born in his family.

Where are his companions; who will rally to help? David looks up to see his longtime friends, now flanking his son (2 Samuel 15–19). And he flees with their taunts ringing into his night: "There is no help for him in God."

His family is shattered, his friends have deserted. His faith has been run through. All that makes life sacred is wrecked.

Selah.

No wonder he stops. The confusion is stifling.

David weighs up the happenings of his history; there's a sudden realization that this isn't the end. His defense is more than a canvas tent. God is steel for him.

And the barrage no longer pierces his soul. His face lifts to the sun. He's at peace.

LORD, how they have iiiiiiiiiiiiiiiiiiiiiiiiiiiiiiiiiiiiiiiiiiiiiiiiiiiiiiiiiii increased who trouble me.

MANY

ARE THEY

who rise up against against me

THERE IS NO HELP FOR HIM IN GOD THERE IS NO

BUT YOU O LORD ARE A SHIELD AROUND ME BUT YOU O LORD ARE A SHIELD AROUND ME BUT YOU O LORD ARE A SHIELD AROUND ME

GLORY

and the One who lifts up my head

The boundary of hope

I cried to the LORD with my voice,
And He heard from His holy hill.
Selah
I lay down and slept;
I awoke, for the LORD sustained me.

PSALM 3, VERSES 4 AND 5

This. Little. Passage.

Our minds are on edge in days of commotion as news feeds clamor through our phones. Global disease leaves us uneasy, land-grabbing rulers throw us off guard. The headlines push our peace about, and we're keenly aware of the miles between us and those we love. And we realize we're small, so very little, with no power to turn things around.

The psalmist is a dad. He is running from his boy. His heart is ruined, his family fractured. He has passed the boundary of hope.

With each phrase of this verse, there is waiting, watching to see if he is heard. Will the Almighty pay attention to him among all the other cries for mercy, all the other pleas for grace?

Stepping into the spaces between the lines of his lament, we find that they are filled with hearing. He's in range of God's ears, God's heart, God's voice. The relief in the midst of this uproar lets him make the most defenseless move: David lies down to sleep.

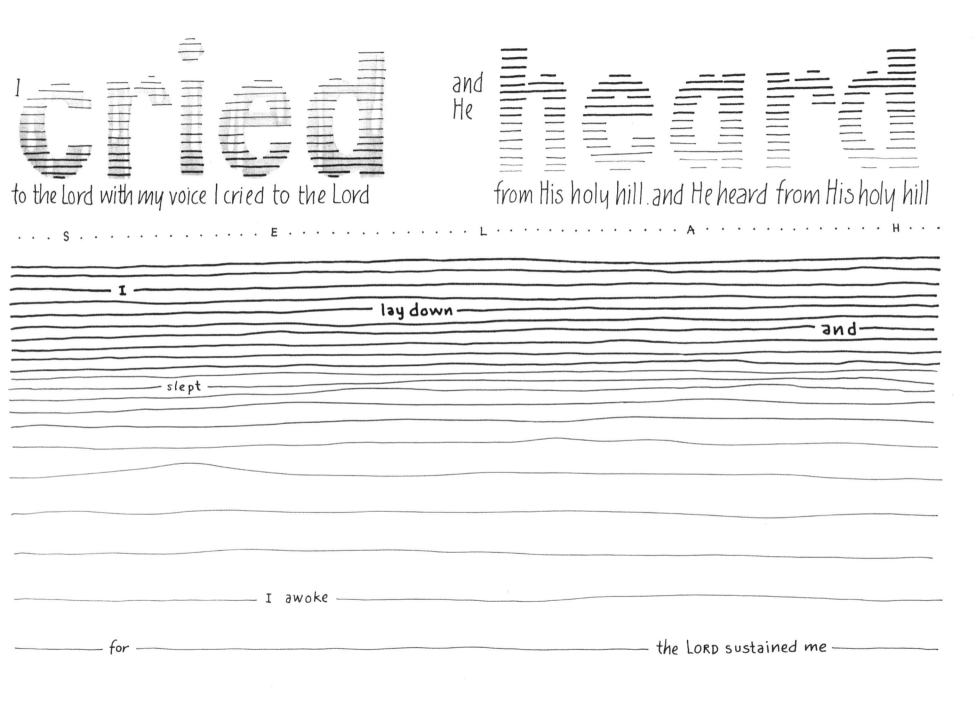

I **cried** to the Lord with my voice I cried to the Lord and He **heard** from His holy hill. and He heard from His holy hill

. . . S . . . . E . . . . L . . . . A . . . . H . . .

I

lay down

and

slept

I awoke

for   the LORD sustained me

Ambushed

I will not be afraid of ten thousands of people
Who have set themselves against me all around.
Arise, O LORD;
Save me, O my God!

PSALM 3, VERSES 6 TO 7A

Being ambushed with no route to escape is the stuff of nightmares. The panic. The whirling around searching for refuge. And then helplessness, and fear.

Feelings of entrapment have resonance in epidemics, in catastrophes, in war. Lost freedoms and restrictions weigh heavily. One Thursday around 8 p.m., in the early days of the pandemic, a noise began outside. Apartment windows opened, and on balconies all around, people cheered and clapped for health workers who were risking their lives to keep us safe. Each Thursday, we went to the window, looking into the eyes of neighbors we couldn't be with. For weeks our community and country joined in the applause. From royalty in palaces to families on welfare, for ten minutes every Thursday, we clapped and wept in powerlessness and thanks. It was deeply moving, this collective lament.

In this little verse, there is stillness where there should be none, right at the center. Thousands have been enlisted by David's son to kill him. He is encircled by dread. Yet, right on the inside of all that is hopeless, he connects to another dimension. He lifts up his voice to stir the Eternal. And in the ambush, he is at peace.

"I will not be afraid."

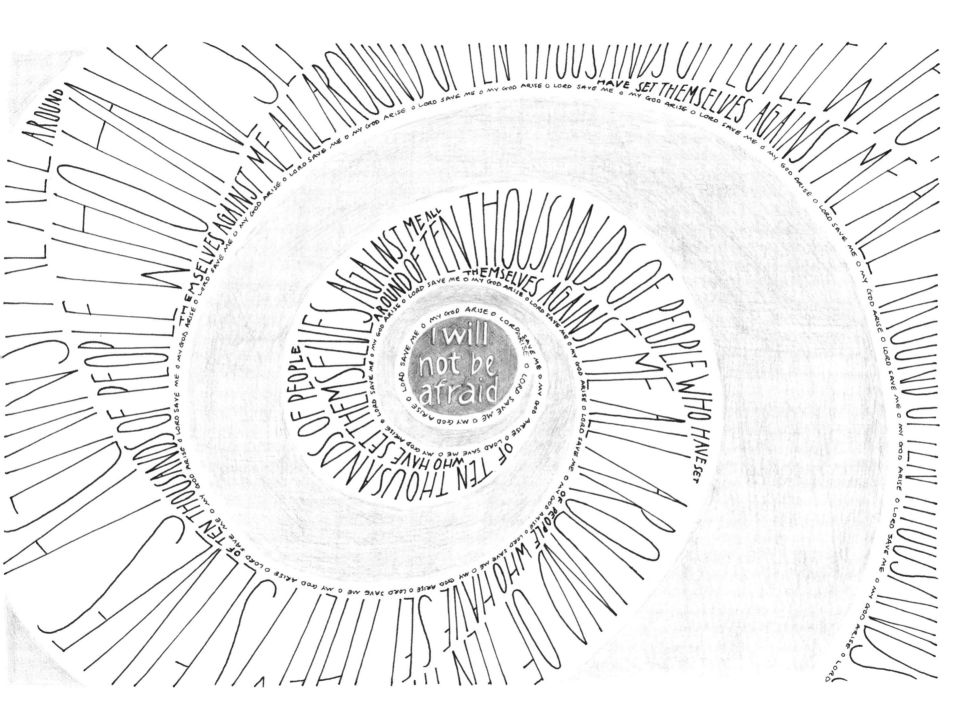

Hand on the gavel

For You have struck all my enemies on the cheekbone;
You have broken the teeth of the ungodly.

PSALM 3, VERSE 7B

There's a burning in the gut when an injustice is done, when wicked people strut away from ruin they have caused with no repercussions for the misery. There's an urge to haul them into the court of humanity to pay in full for the outrage. But atrocity doesn't mean that the guilty get what's coming. And the outrage that stays hidden can drive faith into the mud.

If I'm honest, I'd happily share the judge's bench to help him with his ruling, show him the carnage and lay out all the loss. The gavel's handle is surely long enough for two.

In the lament, the writer cries for God to get up, act, save! Then he leaves justice with Him; he chooses to trust. And in the release of the gavel and exit from the bench, David discovers this ridiculous peace.

Verse 7 is the recollection—he remembers his history, that there was help despite impossible odds. Justice happened. He had seen the proud fall, struck down, teeth broken.

His fear is extinguished at the realization that nothing is hidden, each evil is seen.

And faith breathes.

FOR YOU HAVE

YOU HAVE

ON THE CHEEKBONE

OF THE UNGODLY

Before the end of the story

Salvation belongs to the LORD.
Your blessing is upon Your people.
Selah

PSALM 3, VERSE 8

There should be no words of wonder mid battle. It's inappropriate! The fitting response is terror and resolve. Yet, in the center of his torn-apart world, unable to see family and community, the psalmist calls out about the blessing of God when there is no grace to be seen. He speaks of rescue and serenity before the end of the story. It's baffling.

The middle of a story is not the time to claim peace, yet David does. Is he psyching himself up, trying to overcome panic by projecting success? It is more startling than that.

In remembering how God stepped into his story in the past, he realizes that power doesn't lie with him. His life is in the hands of One who misses nothing. So David lets go of the top job. He steps away from management and finds astonishing release. The responsibility for rescue falls from his shoulders, and in this combat zone, he declares, "Salvation belongs to the LORD." In the middle of it all, he sings out that the blessing of God rests upon a loved humanity.

And here he finds rest. And freedom.

salvation belongs to the LORD salvation belongs to the LORD the LORD salvation belongs to the LORD salvation belongs to the LORD salvation belongs to the LORD salvation belongs to the LORD belongs to the LORD salvation belongs to the LORD salvation belongs to the LORD LORD salvation belongs to the LORD salvation salvation belongs to the LORD salvation belongs to the LORD salvation belongs to the LORD

your blessing be on your people

PEOPLE SELAH.

A Night Prayer of Distress—
A Lament of David

Richard loved his job. He arrived in ministry from a prosperous career and could not be more fulfilled. He quietly encouraged staff through the day, and interns left his office with renewed confidence in their calling. People loitered around him to share news, to discuss dilemmas, to pray; he was present until long after closing time. Richard gave with joy, amazed that the Lord had called him to serve.

If his boss had shamed him for not cleaning his car, he would have held up his hands with, "You're right, I've let that slip." But instead, he said Richard was unapproachable, unsupportive, and self-centered. Richard stumbled to a nearby chair and sat down, dazed.

When the essence of "us" is despised, there begin days of disquiet. How can we be so unobserved? How has our identity been missed? The edges of us seem indistinct, we feel blurred.

When your manager says you're sloppy, but you're king of the spreadsheet; when your partner calls you selfish when all you do is serve; when your *strengths* are brandished as failings, well, that's it. There is nowhere left to go.

Oh, but there is.

This is your psalm.

David is at a loss, pleading for mercy, begging to be heard. It makes sense that he speaks of distress, for in towns where he was loved, there is no welcome. The memory of him has been corrupted with slander and doubt. And he can't fix it. He's at a loss. The joy of him has been rubbed out.

In the midst of this tumbling despair, he stops. There is a Selah, a pause.

David considers—the Almighty had found him in a tight spot before, where he crouched, weakened and small. He remembers the compassion that found him and lifts a quill in the darkness to record the rescue: "You relieved me in my distress." Beautifully, this can also be translated, "You gave me room." I want to paint that in massive letters across all the cramped and crushing places—YOU GAVE ME ROOM. It's the curtains being opened, doors and windows flung wide. It's the strong arm offered to the one in the dark. It's being lifted to the sunlight, stepping into the green. "You gave me room." You made a space for me to stand, to remember who I am, to remove the blur of lies, to strengthen the edges of me.

David rallies, reflective, to consider the crimes—he was crushed by the onslaught, the malice brought him down low. He suggests an appropriate response to match the weight of offense—and goes with "outrage"! "Be angry," he writes. Wait, this is the Bible. There must be a catch, some holy habit to balance things out. Perhaps the chorus of this ancient song will be a memorable self-help list to tell us, count to ten before you speak, or go out for a walk.

But David says anger is right; squashing the pain down into our souls will injure and horribly scar. So, what do we do when pain devastates? Do we blow up and ignore the consequences?

I remember the first time I felt permission to be noisy with my emotions. Adrian and I had been traveling west across northern America and pulled in to a touristy rest stop. There was a big tree to look at in the woods along a path. A truck with a fine collection of state bumper stickers was parked nearby and, as we walked toward the trail, the family returned. Parents with an excited youngster were heading for a vending machine while a scuffling teen, ten paces back, squinted at his phone. We smiled at the family, asking if it was worth the walk. They nodded with, "It's great," and something else I heard only after they'd gone, "Watch out for bears." Bears? It hadn't occurred to me that woods equalled bears. In Scotland, woods equal midges and the occasional deer, not claw-tastic feral beasts. I turned wide-eyed to Adrian as we walked through the undergrowth. It was really quiet. The path opened to a clearing where a huge sign made of metal and set in concrete displayed its graphics of doom! It told us that if a bear came close, to rage, to scream, to jump up and down, to turn all fear into volume. This was not the time for polite conversation, to find a mindfulness app or count to twenty!

David installs a large sign in the landscape of Psalm 4 to make sure we don't miss any moves. He gives us clear details on what we should do—be angry, tremble even, and do not sin. There is space to speak it out, to think it through until there's stillness—to engage, eyes wide with the Almighty. There is room to trust. That's a lot of verbs! David's not calling for passivity.

When lies disorient and make us forget who we are, when our identity is tarnished and we can't be seen, there is a way to stand. Yes, this is your psalm. It leads us into a welcoming space with the One who has been present all along.

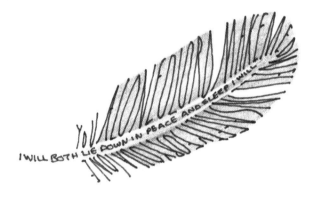

I WILL BOTH LIE DOWN IN PEACE AND SLEEP: FOR THOU LORD ONLY MAKEST ME

Friend or whisperer

Hear me when I call, O God of my righteousness!
You have relieved me in my distress;
Have mercy on me, and hear my prayer.
How long, O you sons of men,
Will you turn my glory to shame?
How long will you love worthlessness
And seek falsehood?
Selah
But know that the LORD has set apart for Himself him
who is godly;
The LORD will hear when I call to Him.

PSALM 4, VERSES 1 TO 3

When menace is upon us, our minds sharpen and are clear. We see right from wrong, safety from danger, and call out strongly for help. Our friends rally around in protective outrage, to defend us and seek our good.

Physical danger was the subject of the previous psalm, where David, surrounded by companions, charged God to get up and act! Yet, in this lament, the request has a wholly different tone. His call is uncertain; he's pleading for an audience, asking for mercy, speaking of distress. *This* crisis has him tormented. Where did his confidence go? What changed?

There is a form of menace that mutilates, that presses down on the soul. When our *character* is questioned, when our strengths and joys are scorned, an internal carnage begins. We cannot see who is a friend and who is whispering lies, and isolation grows. And we reel with the question—is the disappointment of our community echoed in heaven? Will God step back; will He hesitate to listen?

This is David's plight, fighting through gossip for relief in his despair.

And then, as we say in Scotland, he "has a word with himself." He pauses to think. He weighs their scorn and sees the ugliness of their unity. And there is this incredible shift. David rises up as a friend of God, as one who is known and cherished. Whatever is said of his character or deeds, that can fall to the dirt—his identity is held in the safety of heaven. God hasn't stepped back, He is listening.

Heresy in fragments

Be angry, and do not sin.
Meditate within your heart on your bed, and be still.
Selah
Offer the sacrifices of righteousness,
And put your trust in the LORD.

PSALM 4, VERSES 4 AND 5

If you've been around church any length of time, you've likely heard a phrase quoted that allows the just to rage: "Be angry and do not sin." It is found in this lament, but is near useless when cut from its housing, for with only this fragment, we are left with stirred emotion that has no place to go.

But where this phrase lives, there is help and advice, solace, and direction.

Anger at lies and malicious gossip is entirely fitting,[1] but, David urges, *don't engage at this point. It'll likely go quite horribly wrong!* Our move is to our room, and specifically, to our bed. And there, we are to think it through; we're to pause and be very still.

As David writes, he's surrounded by his betrayers, and knows his proposal is a BIG ask; he calls it a "sacrifice"; a cost. We're to face our situation and face the Almighty; to directly engage with both. Everything within us wants to step out of our room and right the wrong, but he calls us in the ugliness of our anger to stay in there with God.

The final appeal is a transfer of ownership of the issue. This is no dismissal of wrong, but an active trust in the justice of the One who heard the slander, clocked the damage, and will not ignore.

A brave process of release.

BE ANGRY

and do not sin . . . and do not sin . . . and do not sin . . . and do not sin . . . and do not sin . . . and do not sin . . . and do not sin . . . and do not sin . . .

e
t
a
t
i
d
e
m

ITH
IN YO
UR HEA
RT ON YO
UR BED WIT
HIN YOUR HEA
RT ON YOUR BED
WITHIN YOUR HEAR
T ON YOUR BED WITH
IN YOUR HEART ON YOU
R BED WITHIN YOUR HEART
ON YOUR BED WITHIN YOUR H
EART ON YOUR BED WITHIN YO
UR HEART ON YOUR BED WITHIN YOU
R HEART ON YOUR BED WITHIN YOUR
HEART ON YOUR BED WITHIN YOUR
ON YOUR BED WITHIN YOUR HEART ON YOUR
BED WITHIN YOUR HEART ON YOUR BED WITHI
N YOUR HEART ON YOUR BED WITHIN YOUR HEART ON YOUR BED WITHIN YOUR HEART ON YOUR BED WITHIN YOUR HEART ON YOUR BED WITHIN YOUR HEART ON YOUR BED WITHIN YOUR HEART ON YOUR BED WITHIN YOUR HEART ON YOUR BED WITHIN YOUR

OFFER THE SACRIFICES OF RIGHTEOUSNESS OFFER THE SACRIFICES OF RIGHTEOUSNESS OFFER THE SACRIFICES OF RIGHTEOUSNESS OFFER THE SACRIFICES OF SACRIFICES OF

PUT YOUR TRUST IN THE LORD AND PUT YOUR TRUST IN THE LORD AND PUT YOUR TRUST IN THE LORD AND PUT YOUR TRUST IN THE LORD AND PUT YOUR TRUST IN THE LORD AND PUT YOUR TRUST IN THE LORD AND PUT YOUR TRUST IN THE LORD AND PUT YOUR TRUST IN THE LORD AND PUT YOUR TRUST IN THE LORD

and be still

Unexpected request

There are many who say,
"Who will show us any good?"
LORD, lift up the light of Your countenance upon us.
You have put gladness in my heart,
More than in the season that their grain and wine
increased.

PSALM 4, VERSES 6 AND 7

Just as the psalmist settled his soul, the naysayers enter with their words of doom. (I drew them in the clouds, bringing in the thunder!) They usher in hopelessness, interpreting his lack of prosperity as a spiteful neglect on God's part. They say that no one is watching and no one cares.

But David just arrived fresh from raw interactions with the Almighty where, in utter defeat, he laid out his rage. And there on his bed, he found only acceptance, tenderness, and friendship.

So, he blocks out their clamor to make his request—for bounty, for crops? Surprisingly not. David asks for something quite unexpected, quite beautiful. He asks the Friend he just wrestled with to raise His head and look at him. He simply calls for Him to glance his way and connect. And the Light that fills David eclipses all gold. He shouts, *"You* have put gladness in my heart," more than joy from the richest harvest!

The ancient writer is overwhelmed by one look from his steady Companion. Friends are the sunshine of life[2]—and this Friend is the supergiant!

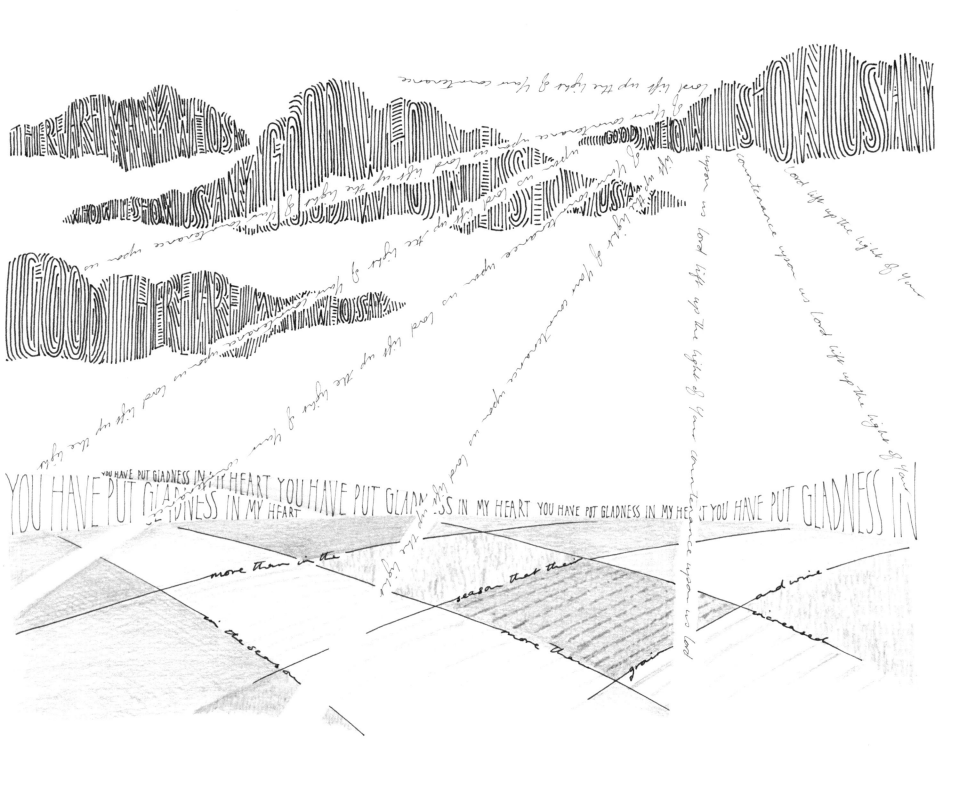

And they lost

I will both lie down in peace, and sleep;
For You alone, O LORD, make me dwell in safety.

PSALM 4, VERSE 8

I love the triumph in this closing phrase. The psalmist emerges from seven verses of inner war. He's gone head to head with venomous companions who've shredded his character before those who matter. With hateful whispering they've undermined his relationships, employing their best efforts to shame and destroy.

And they lost! You kind of want to shout a big, "YES!"

While alone on his bed, defeated and angry, David discovered that the most powerful player in this fierce war was actually the kindest of friends. He found generosity, not accusation; acceptance, not strife. And there was beauty that led him from turmoil to peace.

His identity was not held in the grubby hands of the jealous, but in the eternal hands of God.

Safety where it matters.

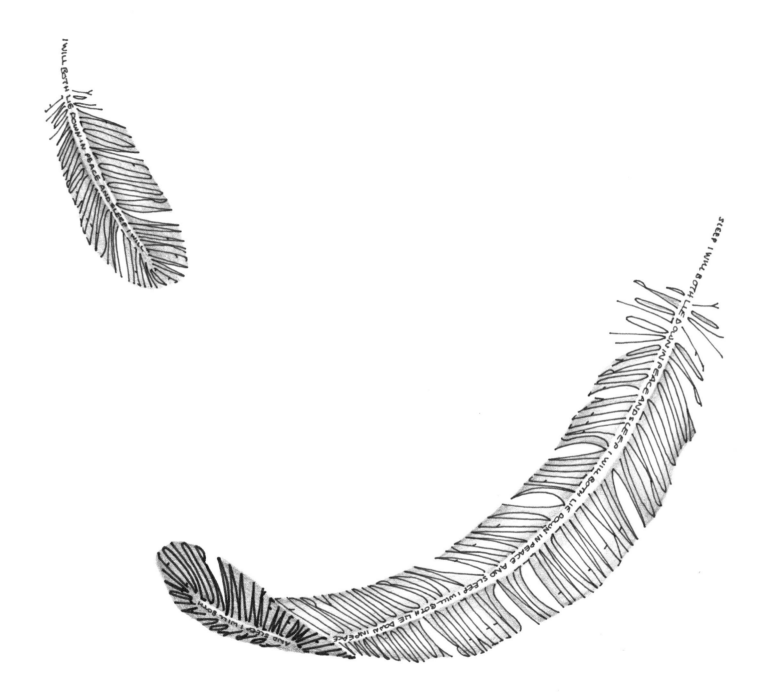

PSALM 5

A Prayer for Direction—
A Lament of David

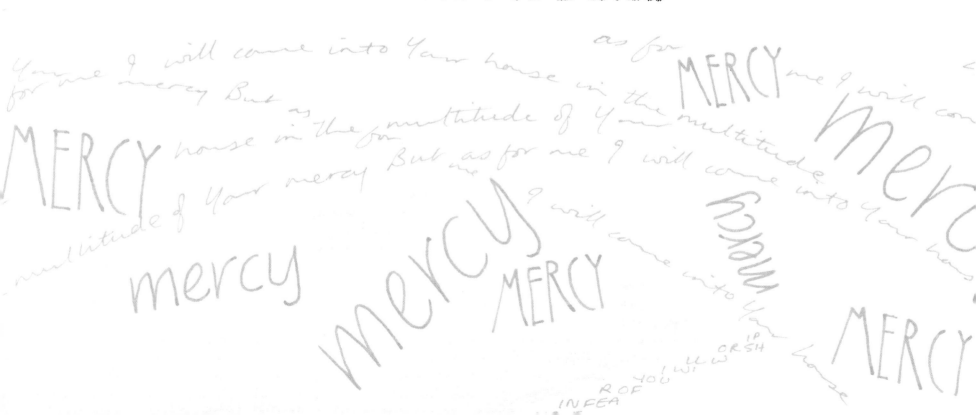

If you were to ask someone you know to hurt someone you hate, you've crossed a line in your relationship; a crisis is now upon you. It's not acceptable to act on our loathings; it goes beyond what is okay. Your friend might grip your shoulder and sit you down with frowns and tea to chart a different path through the misery that won't send you both to jail!

This poem is the record of frowns and tea, the notes from an uncomfortable meeting. The psalmist asked somebody huge to be part of his fight, to demolish the men who threw him out of his home. He asks to be rescued from the borderlands and brought back into his life.

But before David asks for help in his quest, he marks out all the players. He needs to have it straight: who is who and what is what.

Who is God?

What is evil?

These ultimate questions must be answered before he can move forward with his plan.

He begins with: Who is God? Identifying the divine seems fairly key in the embracing of any creed. To know who we worship bounds our days; it gives space for flow, and margins for fear.

"What comes into your mind when you think about God is the most important thing about your life," wrote theologian A. W. Tozer.[1] So what springs to mind: Who is He?

If the Almighty is indifferent, His followers will be confused; if angry, they will be afraid. If He is judgmental, they'll hide and pretend; and if disappointed, they will fill their lives with good works to try and earn His favor. Who *is* the God our lives are oriented toward?

The poet spends a quarter of the psalm weighing up what God is like. It is his first question, and its answer determines all the other questions. Relationships, career, priorities—

every dimension of our living is shaped by who we worship, by who God the Father is. Every dimension of our living is shaped by who we worship, by who God the Father *is*.

Father's Day was coming up, and Jack had worked on a card all morning. Blue glitter framed the carefully chosen photo. He wanted Sunday to be perfect. The strong footsteps padding around the house late last night told him Dad was back from work travels. Father's Day was going to be great.

Jack woke early to make breakfast, filling a favorite mug with tea, as cornflakes softened in a bowl on the tray. Beaming, he crossed the tiles holding a stripey blue plate topped with buttered toast. But hearing his dad's footsteps by the door, Jack jumped up in a jumble of fright. The plate slipped from his hand and then hit the floor, splintering into ceramic and toast triangles. The forlorn little boy looked up from the mess.

What now?

The reactions of many fathers flit into view. In the supermarket, we've seen a dad's anger explode on a child, or we've winced at a father's disdain. But we've also seen dads rush to lift children out of the trouble, enveloping all the upset in their arms.

We have watched so many responses to the same sorts of messes. And they hinge on the character of the father, not the behavior of the child.

What about our blunders when considering the Eternal Father?

We could shatter the plate, smash the window, or set the whole house ablaze. The Father will do what the Father will do, independent of the actions we take. It wholly depends on the nature of the Father.

The psalmist makes a list as he prepares to approach the Almighty in the early dawn light. He watches God's actions, writes down what he sees in an attempt to grasp His nature. He can't find words big enough to say who God is, so writes down what He is not—*You have nothing to do with what's vile, or evil, or base. You have nothing to do with lies or what's cruel or devious. You have nothing to do with those who are proud or in any way unjust.*[2]

By finding out what isn't, he found out what is.

You're a God who inhabits goodness; virtue has its home in You. The humble can rest at Your side. Truth tellers are free; the peaceful and honest can be at home with You for that is who You are.

He finds stillness with God in the thick of the action. He is lifted out of trouble by the Eternal's strong arms. His heart is at peace, and he starts to sing out this stunning portrayal of God.

He has addressed the question of God and now turns to the question of evil. David's eye scans the encroaching watchers; he notes their actions and maps out what he sees. The wickedness they harbor swells up from a deep place; it gushes in mockery from their mouths. All around him are those infected with a spreading unease. Their lies destroy life, contaminate relationships, and removed him further from his family and home.

David has come to the edge of things and from this place comes his plea: *God, step into my fight. Throw them into a sea of their own crimes, let them be immersed in the evil they* endorse. *This wrong is against You.* He asks God to hurt them. Walter Brueggeman wrote: "It is an act of profound faith to entrust one's most precious hatreds to God knowing they will be taken seriously."[3] His words express more than hot emotion; they express a burning faith.

As David looks around, he realizes that he doesn't stand alone. He's surrounded by a community whose fierce trust is in God. And he says what he sees from this place of faith: God will bless; God will favor; He will cover the community of the righteous in joy.

Here, he rests. God is entreated, evil is outlined, and the poet is at peace.

LEAD ME O LORD
BECAUSE OF MY ENEMIES
RIGHTEOUSNESS
IN YOUR
LEAD ME O LORD

Where air is thin

Give ear to my words, O LORD,
Consider my meditation.
Give heed to the voice of my cry,
My King and my God,
For to You I will pray.
My voice You shall hear in the morning, O LORD;
In the morning I will direct it to You,
And I will look up.

PSALM 5, VERSES 1 TO 3

It is early morning, 1000 BC. Rays of sunshine split the coldness of the desert night as disorientation blazes in. Thoughts resume their well-worn tracks, searching for answers, oasis, relief. Sleep hasn't eased the family heartache, and peace is as elusive as water in the sand.

King David's sunrise cry asks God to pay attention, to hear beyond what's audible and grasp the grit of his pain. And, he makes it clear, he is going nowhere—this is the call that will waken each dawn.

As David's cry filled my senses, I found myself laying down the image that fills my mind when I pray. Before words are uttered, I step silently toward the throne room doors. They stand unguarded, a fraction open. They stretch as high as the Mordor gates, holding all of the awe and none of the dread. I slip into the vast room; it is cool here at the back. My eyes are transfixed on light far ahead. There on the throne sits the Ancient of Days, blazing in light, high above. With trembling joy I approach. I sense His welcome, feel the warmth of His smile.

Each of us calls out to Him from somewhere. There is a point where we meet. What image fills your senses? Where do you talk? Are you in a booth in a diner, on the glowing rings of Saturn, in a whitewashed cave, a pulsing void? This is no idle daydream; it is a place of sacred communion where air is thin, where Mystery and mortal touch. What a magnificent wonder in our ordinary days.

and I will look up and I will look up and I will look up and I will look up and I will look up and I

and I will look up

and I will look up

and I will look up

and I will look up

IN THE MORNING I WILL DIRECT IT TO YOU IN THE MORNING I WILL DIRECT IT TO YOU IN THE MORNING I WILL DIRECT IT TO YOU IN THE MORNING I WILL DIRECT IT TO YOU IN THE MORNING I WILL DI

WORDS O LORD CONSIDER MY MEDITATION GIVE HEED TO THE VOICE OF MY CRY GIVE EAR TO MY WORDS O LORD

CONSIDER MY MEDITATION GIVE HEED TO THE VOICE OF MY CRY GIVE EAR TO MY WORDS O LORD CONSIDER MY MEDITATION GIVE HEED TO THE VOICE OF MY CRY GIVE EAR TO MY WORDS O LORD

WORDS O LORD CONSIDER MY MEDITATION GIVE HEED TO THE VOICE OF MY CRY GIVE EAR TO MY WORDS O LORD CONSIDER MY MEDITATION GIVE HEED TO THE VOICE OF MY CRY GIVE EAR TO

IN THE MORNING I WILL DIRECT IT TO YOU IN THE MORNING I WILL DIRECT IT TO YOU IN THE MORNING I WILL DIRECT IT TO YOU IN THE MORNING I WILL DIRECT IT TO YOU INT

GIVE EAR TO MY WORDS O LORD CONSIDER MY MEDITATION GIVE HEED TO THE VOICE OF MY CRY GIVE EAR TO MY WORDS O LORD

MY KING AND MY GOD MY KING AND MY GOD MY KING AN

FOR TO YOU I WILL PRAY FOR TO YOU I WILL PRAY FOR TO YOU I

MY VOICE YOU SHALL HEAR IN THE MORNING O LORD

Night and day

For You are not a God who takes pleasure in wickedness,
Nor shall evil dwell with You.
The boastful shall not stand in Your sight;
You hate all workers of iniquity.
You shall destroy those who speak falsehood;
The LORD abhors the bloodthirsty and deceitful man.

PSALM 5, VERSES 4 TO 6

We sat with David in his dawn encounter, pondering his thoughts. He invited God to meet him where the ache lay, deep in unspoken parts of him (verses 1–3). His gaze remains on the Eternal as night loosens its grip of the skies and the sun takes charge from the gloom.

David turns from the beauty of looking up (verse 3), to the reality of his plight. Those advancing toward him to do great harm are as different from his God as night is from the day:

- while boasters thunder in the distance, the Almighty has come close.

- while his weaponized son storms in shadows, he is settled in light.

- and while deceivers and liars revel in malice, David is enveloped in the steadiness of his Maker.

The contrasts are startling.

And we sense his whole being pull toward Goodness, where radiance obliterates the night; where the soul is at rest.

Waiting for rain

But as for me, I will come into Your house in the
multitude of Your mercy;
In fear of You I will worship toward Your holy temple.
Lead me, O LORD, in Your righteousness because of my
enemies;
Make Your way straight before my face.

PSALM 5, VERSES 7 AND 8

Is this the point where the warrior king bristles, separating himself from lesser mortals and reckoning the quality of his worship distinguishes him from the rabble? Is he building up to smugness, detailing the shortcomings of others? That's what we may expect, but it isn't the posture we find.

David writes of mercy.

We used to live near Cambridge, where soft fields stretched out the horizons. Summers were glorious with hot, dry days that could run into weeks. While I was all joyful freckles, the farmers in our community grew quieter. Soil hardened to endless clay; crops were stunted, livelihoods on hold. The ministers in the town gave voice to the silence, "Have mercy, Lord. Send rain." We waited more and spoke less. Until one day in thunderous beauty it came, pouring down hope, rebuilding families, releasing tension. And in the deluge, everything flowed, joyful chatter, dreams for the future. This multitude of mercy, this kindness.

David's stance was not swaggering self-righteousness, scorning the wicked to make them look small. He had lived through many days and knew that evil was not far from his soul. So he came with gratitude, relying on mercy, asking help for his steps and companionship for his life.

We live in no monochrome world, where "we're" good and "they're" bad. Our hearts can be shadowed, our trust misaligned, and *yet*, there is mercy.

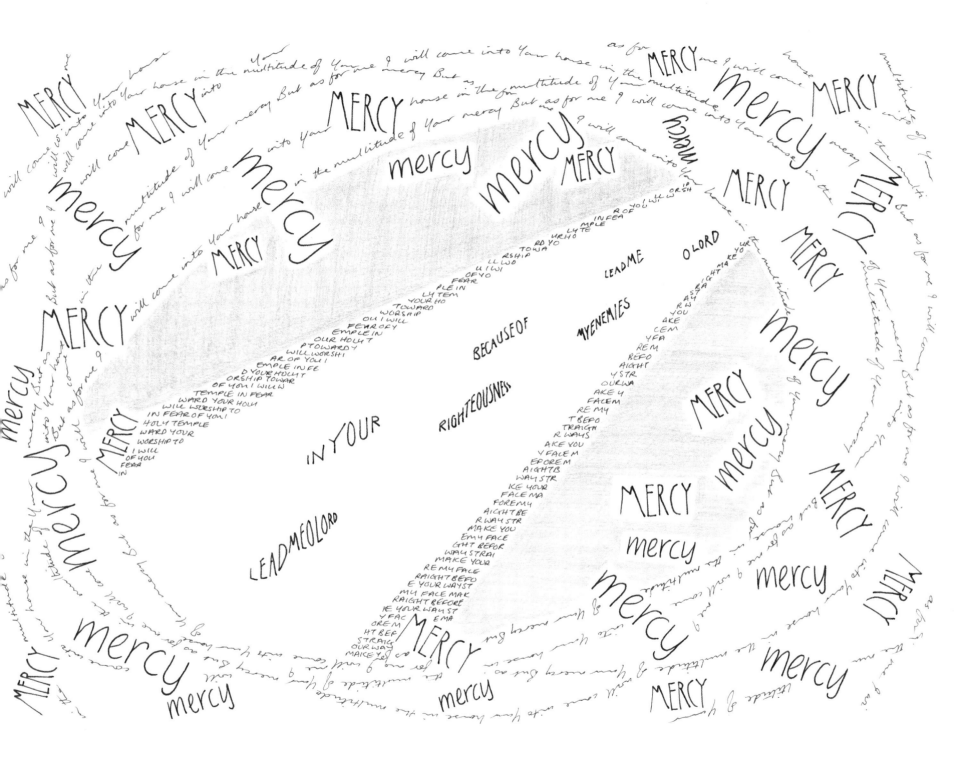

Dead men walking

For there is no faithfulness in their mouth;
Their inward part is destruction;
Their throat is an open tomb;
They flatter with their tongue.
Pronounce them guilty, O God!
Let them fall by their own counsels;
Cast them out in the multitude of their transgressions,
For they have rebelled against You.
PSALM 5, VERSES 9 AND 10

There was a moment, speaking at a retreat a while back where I asked those present what they'd like God to do to those who'd caused them great harm. A number of faces turned to the ceiling while mouthing the word "lightning." You could not fail to be moved by the pain: stolen relationships, childhoods, vocations, the palpable grief of the wounded stirred in silent wrath. We all get it.

And we wonder what was wished for, for the guilty in the Bronze Age. Perhaps David's approach to his terrorizers would run louder, with death to the evil and strength to the good. It would surely be cruder than our civilized whispered reserve.

But his rhetoric is not that. There is nuance and consideration. He knew that the power to obliterate was available (verses 4–6), which makes his request a puzzle.

Instead of calling for slaughter, the ancient thinker examines his persecutors. He stands at the point where their two worlds meet and studies the soundtrack between them—he analyzes the audio. And his assessment? He hears their mouths spew out lies from writhing resentments; their tongues, deceit from a deeper decay. They're rotting from the inside—they're dead men walking.

He appeals for no plagues to obliterate or fire to consume. His request is measured and mournful. *God, they have chosen their code—let them fall by it. They have pursued this path, banish them to its end.*

He walks from the exchange, steps out of the scene. These crimes will be settled in the realm of eternity; he is released.

PRONOUNCE THEM GUILTY O GOD

FOR THEY HAVE REBELLED AGAINST YOU FOR THEY HAVE REBELLED AGAINST YOU FOR THEY HAVE REBELLED AGAINST YOU FOR THEY HAVE REBELLED

them

let

fall

OPEN TOMB

DESTRUCTION

FAITHFULNESS

LET THEM FALL BY THEIR OWN COUNSELS CAST THEM OUT IN THE MULTITUDE OF THEIR TRANSGRESSIONS LET THEM FALL

Volume spike

But let all those rejoice who put their trust in You;
Let them ever shout for joy, because You defend them;
Let those also who love Your name
Be joyful in You.

PSALM 5, VERSE 11

The first footprint on the path to freedom isn't mobilizing a multitude behind a cause. It starts with an echo, a DNA memory, some hunger for paradise when all was at rest.

As I drew the image, the verse split into two. Trust in God and love for His name came before all the noise. Erwin McManus captures it: "In order to be ready for battle, you must first know peace."[4] David's reliance on the Almighty carried peace to his core. And on the inside, right in the center, all was well. He was accepted, defended. And from this place of rest, hope could unfurl.

The ancient warrior had paid attention to the audio. He'd heard the bitter tones of his foes (verses 9–10), and now he tunes in to pick up on the sounds of peace. And this is the brilliant bit: what he hears isn't whale music from soft slo-mo feeds. He is surrounded by shouting! Raucous, joyous, uninhibited sound bursts alive from the stillness.

You roar when the elation of your heart eclipses the self-consciousness of your soul. The ridiculous win, the cleared debt, the invitation to the palace—something stunning. That's when the shout gets out, when the volume spikes.

And that's where David is. At a meeting of souls, accepted by Wonder. From a place of peace bursts a shout of triumph. And it's loud.

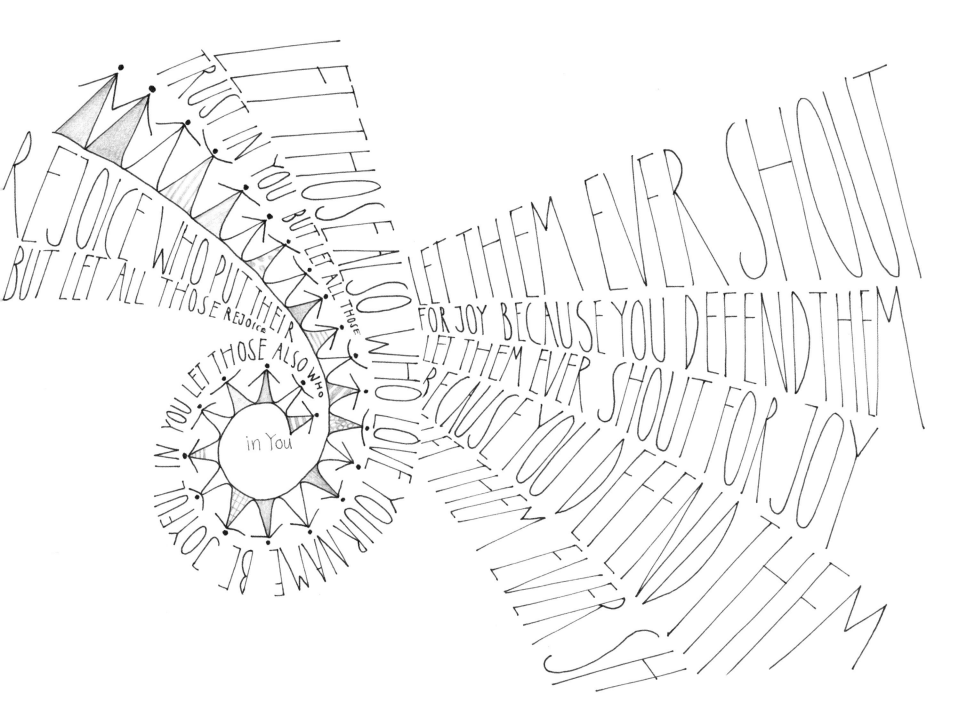

Personal protective equipment

For You, O LORD, will bless the righteous;
With favor You will surround him as with a shield.

PSALM 5, VERSE 12

From the refuge of their communion, where peace has birthed joy (verse 11), the lyrics move into battle vocabulary. Our warrior-poet takes a look at what the well-equipped fighter is wearing. The right gear counts on the field, for without good equipment, people fall in the fray.

Before 2020, most of us didn't know what PPE stood for. After the pandemic, how could anyone not know about personal protective equipment? Green gowns and face shields filled our news feeds, images of shaken medics were etched into our minds. Those stopping the advance and guarding our families needed the right kit, since going into this battle ill-equipped meant disease or even death.

David writes of the need for protection, of a doubling of effort for the good to be safe. He says that two pieces of armor are needed for courage: one is *blessing* and the other, *favor*. Yet, three thousand years have clouded their meaning and switched "blessing" for comfort and "favor" for cash.

Blessing: that enfolding stillness of the eternal Defender, the essential tone before battle begins. And favor: a shield, this extra kit, the protective kindness of armor over armor. This spiritual PPE kit comes from One who knows the war, who's with us in the thick of it.

Blessing and favor, an inside/outside thing. A double promise for a life of peace.

the righteous

A Prayer for Mercy—
A Penitential Lament of David

The playground bully carves "You are nothing" into the unset concrete of our identity; but within the hour, in Grandma's kitchen, "You are my sunshine" is pressed into the gray. A network of relationships are built into our lives to give us the definition of "me." We're called lazy, then kind; sensitive, and then selfish. We are marked by every encounter—with imprints that speak of welcome, and incisions to say we do not belong.

And just as we settle into our solidifying self, culture blusters in. In the 1980s we were taught to "believe in yourself"; self-esteem was crucial to happiness. In the early 2000s, we needed to embrace self-help; a therapeutic approach was vital because the past defined us. A decade later, we learned to leave our shame and rise; the route to success required empathy, as we were all victims. Each decade reached for new ways to be whole.

We grew tired of feeling unfinished, so we sculpted a life of flawless days. Our online exhibits were entrancing, the filters charmed, and each crafted label convinced others of our soaring joy. And in the new religion of fame, we diminished. We became a mystery to our community, a stranger to ourselves. We became the unknown.

Why all the focus on identity?

Because something is happening in this psalm that is central to self-actualization. This type of poem occurs seven times in the one hundred and fifty. It has to do with penitence.

The philosopher Augustine speaks from fourth-century Algeria: "Grant Lord that I may know myself, that I may know Thee."[1] In the 1500s in France, reformer John Calvin continues the theme: "There is no deep knowing of God without a deep knowing of self. And no deep knowing of self without a deep knowing of God."[2]

Why do theologians of such note place value on self-knowledge? Isn't putting "me" in the frame a marker for pride? Surely, the goal of a Christian is to focus on God.

You know, "He must increase and I must decrease"—it's Sunday school stuff.

I wonder if an idea has crept into Christendom that anything less than eradicating self triggers eye rolls in heaven. That understanding the self is psycho-pop weakness and our gaze should center on God alone.

If denial of self is the marker for sainthood, the psalmist fails dismally. In this ten-verse reflection, he uses the personal pronoun twenty times!

Does he use it to showcase his glittering life, to tell about crowds roaring his praise? No, his time is spent in solitude and examination. He encounters his vilest, contemptible self. He reckons there's much to be angry about, plenty for God to condemn. We hear no excuses or claims of innocence. David invites God into his soul's uncovering. And in deep awareness of who he is, of what he has done, he cries for pardon. He needs a God with a spine who cares about the harm he has caused; he needs Someone who is capable of forgiveness.

I'd been invited again to join the group of atheist scholars, gathered on this wet, Sunday afternoon. We crossed the cobbles and ducked through the door of the sixteenth-century café. As more gathered, the seats were arranged so that everyone was included. The wingback chairs and cast-iron stove all evoked smiles and nodding heads. Someone mentioned their family's roast dinners and memories mixed in with the cozy mood. Menus were studied, orders made, as we settled into the scene; this was lovely.

In the quiet, someone spoke: "I miss feeling clean. After messing up a week, I'd go to church on Sunday, and I left feeling clean. I miss that." I waited for expletives and witty disdain, as mentions of church often roused rawness and contempt. But on this quiet Sunday, no one spoke. The vulnerability was left suspended in the air. As we stared into the fire, the lament was repeated, "I miss feeling clean."

It was as if I was sitting in the nave at a service of remembrance, a eulogy stirring memories of the one who had gone. It was a moving and holy exchange, a tribute to being known and being forgiven. A waitress stepped into the space, carrying orders. "Whose is the beetroot salad? And the bread and olives?" It was over.

There is something we need. It's deep within us. When we find ourselves at midnight seeking cover for our shame, there is One who moves toward us, calling us beloved.

And there is pardon. And we can be clean.

my soul is greatly troubled my soul is greatly troubled my soul is greatly troubled my soul is greatly troubled my soul

but You O Lord – how long? but You O Lord – how long? But You O Lord – how long? But You O Lord – how long? But You O Lord – how long? But You

return O Lord, deliver me return O Lord, deliver me return O Lord, deliver me save me for Your mercy's sake O save me troubled my soul is greatly troubled my soul

return O Lord – deliver me return O Lord for Your mercy's sake O save me

The silent brawl

O LORD, do not rebuke me in Your anger,
Nor chasten me in Your hot displeasure.
Have mercy on me, O LORD, for I am weak;
O LORD, heal me, for my bones are troubled.
My soul also is greatly troubled;
But You, O LORD—how long?

PSALM 6, VERSES 1 TO 4

This poem may have struggled on ancient social media. There are no fine scenes, noble friends, or shining chariots; the picture is grainy and the atmosphere tarnished.

We enter the psalmist's bedchamber in the night watches. The room lies thick with questions, crammed with doubts.

Here, too, is where our silent brawls take place, where battle is done. We lie uneasy, dissecting our hurts, reviewing our regrets. And in these dark scuffles we wonder if the snags in our days are penance for some unknown fault, an inner flaw. And with dawn comes hope that the turmoil stays hidden, we must maintain decorum, smile our way through the day. Gloomy sharing doesn't fit with our profiles of purpose!

But David doesn't choose silence, nor ask us for pity. He takes a step toward courage. "What is the bravest thing you've ever said?" asks the boy in Charlie Mackesy's book. "'Help,' said the horse."[3]

David cries, *Help!* He allows the torment to move him. With broken sentences, bereft and small, he calls out to remain in the land of the living, to walk through the shadows in the care of his Friend.

What a comfort that this night is included in his song, that there's no bright filter to mask out the gray.

Keeping the audio

Return, O LORD, deliver me!
Oh, save me for Your mercies' sake!
For in death there is no remembrance of You;
In the grave who will give You thanks?

PSALM 6, VERSE 5

When all the funeral sandwiches and kind friends had gone, the thing about the house was the silence. Sure, loved ones live on in our memories, but there's no audio with the recollection. Mum would laugh on the phone with her sisters and sing when she went around the house; and Dad was always calling her, about where this or that was as he settled into his tasks. These simple things were silent.

David has clearly done something that he thinks deserves God's judgment, for his pleading for mercy is intense. And the lever he uses for convincing the Lord? He speaks of their relationship and conversation: *Lord, the worship You hear with every dawn, if You smite me, that will be gone.* He asks God to keep their relationship going, to let him stay in the frame. Dead bodies can't speak; they can't sing, they can't thank. The friendship would lie with David, cold in the earth.

So he asks that he would not be silenced by death, that the audio track could run on.

It's a gutsy request!

For in death for in death for in death for in death for in death

in the grave who will give You thanks?

Towels not tissues

I am weary with my groaning;
All night I make my bed swim;
I drench my couch with my tears.
My eye wastes away because of grief;
It grows old because of all my enemies.

PSALM 6, VERSES 6 AND 7

David, how? How did you end up in this place? Aren't you the bear-mauling, lion-killing, giant-slaying shepherd boy wonder—the curly haired superhero with Michelangelo muscles in the picture-Bible pages? How can you win against armies and then wail through the night; how can you beat up monsters and then sob in the dark? Just how? Those rivals didn't leave you floundering like this.

I think the answer may lie in the space *between* the players.

Between a bear and a shepherd there is no connection. The shepherd is not seeking consent for the path of his life. The roles are in order; he's simply guarding his livelihood.

The space between them is without expectation; the loss of the bear is the shepherd's gain.

Between a giant and a fighter, it's much the same. The space between them lies arid. There's no bond to sever or blessing to forfeit, only safety is in sight. The giant's doom is the fighter's freedom. There is nothing to lose.

But the one he wrestles in his room on this darkest night is the object of David's faith. This "opponent" is his Companion, his steadier, his strength. The unfiltered space between them is everything. It is where David lives, where he's accepted. Mauled by questions and ravaged by doubt, he lies trembling, turned to water. He believes his Friend has walked away (verses 1–5), that he has lost the connection.

And pain is transmitted across three thousand years to the silent brawls of our own night watches.

There are spaces between that matter.

BED SWIM ALL

ALL NIGHT I MAKE MY COUCH I RED TO SWIM ALL NIGHT.

I am weary with my groaning

I am weary with my groaning I am weary

IT GROWS OLD BECAUSE OF MY ENEMIES

I am weary with my groaning

MY EYE WASTES AWAY BECAUSE WITH ALL NIGHT I MAKE MY BED SWIM

ALL NIGHT I MAKE MY BED SWIM

I DRENCH MY COUCH BECAUSE OF MY COUCH

BECAUSE OF GRIEF MY

IT GROWS OLD BECAUSE OF

MY EYE WAS: I DRENCH MY COUCH WITH TEARS

BECAUSE OF ALL OF MY ENEMIES

BECAUSE OF ALL OF MY ENEMIES

I am weary with my groaning I am weary with my groaning

I am weary with my groaning I am weary with my groaning I am weary with my

I with my groaning I am weary with my groaning I am weary with my groaning I am weary with my groaning

Bring tea . . .

I am weary with my groaning;
All night I make my bed swim;
I drench my couch with my tears.
My eye wastes away because of grief;
It grows old because of all my enemies.

PSALM 6, VERSES 6 AND 7

When a friend is in pain, we can be conflicted. There's hesitation, concern, and doubt: "I don't know what to say. What if I get it wrong?"

But loved ones who are hurt are not looking for greeting card platitudes. They don't need our eloquence; they need us to be close, to pause our schedules, take out the earbuds, ditch the phone and the shades, and show up, unmasked. Human.

With tea.

(You may have spotted that the passage above is the same as the page before. I've found over the years of meditation, that some verses don't let you move on. They're not done with you when the picture is over. They demand more attention, more pondering, more time.)

I AM WEARY WITH MY GROANING I AM WEARY WITH MY GROANING I AM WEARY WITH MY GROANING I AM WEARY WITH MY GRO
ALL NIGHT I MAKE MY BED SWIM ALL NIGHT I MAKE MY BED SWIM ALL NIGHT I MAKE MY BED SWIM ALL NIGHT I
I DRENCH MY COUCH WITH MY TEARS I DRENCH MY COUCH WITH MY TEA
MY EYE WASTES AWAY BECAUSE OF GRIEF MY EYE WASTES AWAY BECAUSE OF
IT GROWS OLD BECAUSE OF MY ENEMIES IT GROWS OLD BECAUSE OF MY ENEMIES IT GROWS OLD

I AM WEARY WITH MY GROANING I AM WEARY WITH MY GROANING I AM WEARY WITH
ALL NIGHT I MAKE MY BED SWIM ALL NIGHT I MAKE MY BED SWIM ALL NIGHT
I DRENCH MY COUCH WITH MY TEARS I DRENCH MY COUCH WITH MY
MY EYE WASTES AWAY BECAUSE OF GRIEF
IT GROWS OLD BECAUSE OF MY ENEMIES IT GROWS OLD BECAUSE OF MY ENEMIES IT GROWS OLD

I AM WEARY WITH MY GROANING I AM WEARY WITH MY GROANING I AM WEARY
ALL NIGHT I MAKE MY BED SWIM ALL NIGHT I MAKE MY BED
I DRENCH MY COUCH WITH MY TEARS I DRENCH MY COUCH WITH MY TEARS I DR

I AM WEARY WITH MY GROANING I AM WEARY WITH MY GROANING I AM
ALL NIGHT I MAKE MY BED SWIM ALL
I DRENCH MY CO

I AM WEARY WITH MY GROANING I AM WEARY WITH MY GROANING I AM WEARY WITH
ALL NIGHT I MAKE MY BED SWIM ALL N
I DRENCH MY

I AM WEARY WITH MY GROANING I AM WEARY WITH MY GROANING I AM WEARY WITH
ALL NIGHT I MAKE MY BED SWIM ALL NIGHT I MAKE MY BED SWIM
I DRENCH MY COUCH WITH

I AM WEARY WITH MY GROANING I AM WEARY WITH MY GROANING I AM WEARY WITH
ALL NIGHT I MAKE MY BED SWIM ALL NIGHT I MAKE MY BED SWIM ALL NIGHT I MAKE MY BED SWIM A
I DRENCH MY COUCH WITH MY TEARS I DRENCH MY COUCH WITH MY TEARS I DRENCH
MY EYE WASTES AWAY BECAUSE OF GRIEF MY EYE WASTES AWAY BECAUSE OF
IT GROWS OLD BECAUSE OF MY ENEMIES IT GROWS OLD BECAUSE OF MY ENEMIES IT GROWS OLD

I AM WEARY WITH MY GROANING I AM WEARY WITH MY GROANING I AM WEARY WITH
ALL NIGHT I MAKE MY BED SWIM ALL NIGHT I MAKE MY BED SWIM ALL NIGHT I MAKE MY BED
I DRENCH MY COUCH WITH MY TEARS I DRENCH MY COUCH WITH MY TEARS I DRENCH MY
MY EYE WASTES AWAY BECAUSE OF GRIEF MY EYE WASTES AWAY BECAUSE OF GRIEF MY EYE WASTES AWAY BECAUSE OF GRIEF MY EYE
WASTES AWAY BECAUSE

I AM WEARY WITH MY GROANING I AM WEARY WITH MY GROANING I AM WEARY WITH MY GROANING I AM
ALL NIGHT I MAKE MY BED SWIM ALL NIGHT I MAKE MY BED SWIM ALL NIGHT I MAKE MY BED SWIM ALL
I DRENCH MY COUCH WITH MY GROANING I AM WEARY WITH MY GROANING I AM WEARY WITH MY GROANING I AM WEARY WITH
MY TEARS I DRENCH MY COUCH WITH MY TEARS I DRENCH MY COUCH WITH MY TEARS I DRENCH

. . . and cake!

I am weary with my groaning;
All night I make my bed swim;
I drench my couch with my tears.
My eye wastes away because of grief;
It grows old because of all my enemies.

PSALM 6, VERSES 6 AND 7

The night's anguish has left him drained. He lies on the far side of hope. The contrast with David, the painted Sunday school warrior, is unsettling. These lines seldom get much of an airing, for they are raw, exposed, unsafe.

Surely, we should not allow the questions of the night to creep into the pages of the day.

But these echoes, this anguish, are etched into his soul. He cannot keep it inside.

Here we sit with him. For what is needed in sorrow is presence. And tea. And later, there may be a need for cake!

(This passage is the same as the last two. It held on for a little longer.)

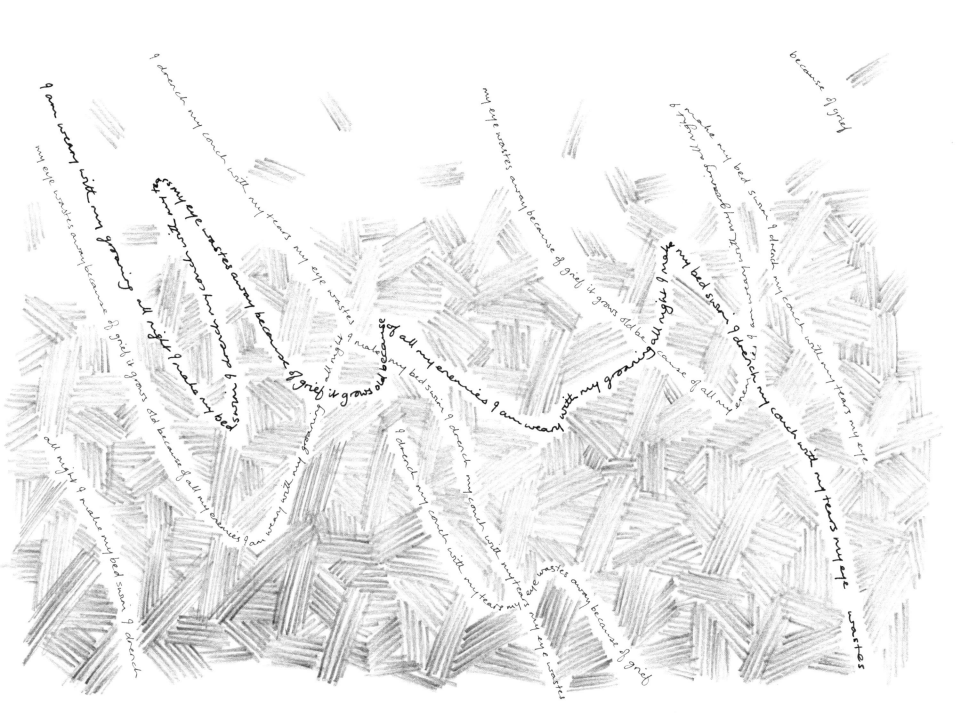

Voldemort to Vader

Depart from me, all you workers of iniquity;
For the LORD has heard the voice of my weeping.
The LORD has heard my supplication;
The LORD will receive my prayer.
Let all my enemies be ashamed and greatly troubled;
Let them turn back and be ashamed suddenly.

PSALM 6, VERSES 8 TO 10

"The best remedy for us against an evil man is a long space between us both,"[4] said Charles Spurgeon. One hundred years of Hollywood concurs, the distance between the goodies and the baddies is where the tension rings. From Voldemort to Vader, it is the narrative we pay for—that good will triumph, and villains will be crushed (most satisfyingly in front of those they torment!). *This* is what David is asking for.

As he moves into the day he has taken an audit of the people in his life. He sees the haters: those who've blasted his hopes, the rivals who've plotted his downfall. They, he declares, can go.

He straightens his back and studies the facts: all their vileness and scorn have not altered his value. He is heard, not rejected, by his steadying Friend. He is held, not condemned.

So he prays for their deeds to be unmasked in the sight of the community. He prays, not for them to be flattered, but shamed. For them to feel an intense revulsion of their very selves. And for that distress to be the trigger to send them bolting, heads covered, disturbed by who they are.

David stands tall, strong. His cause is seen, his plight is heard.

A Meditation about Slander—
A Lament of David

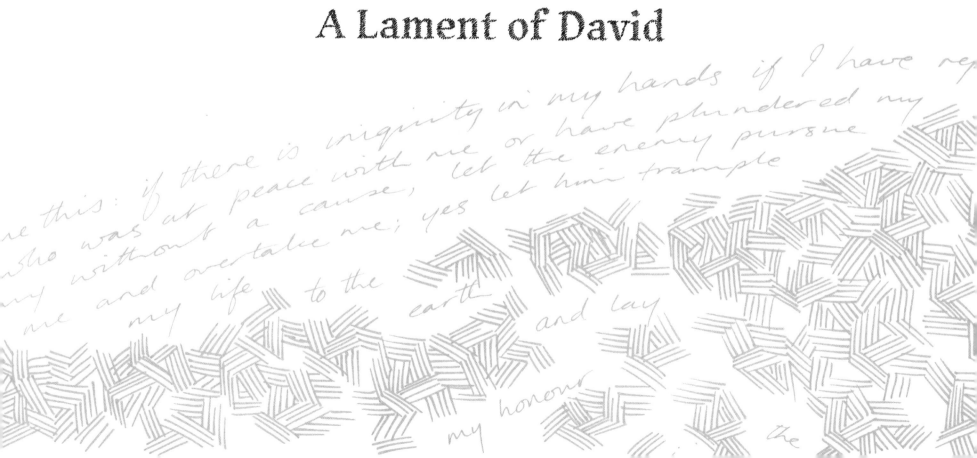

"It is the fashion nowadays to decry the clergy," said the old vicar in Agatha Christie's *Tuesday Club Murders*.[1] If Agatha were to wander into many of our places of worship, she may encounter another trend. It is the fashion nowadays to decry the self, to view joy and confidence as foolishness and pride. For followers of God should surely be grave; there is much to be solemn about. Perhaps the following conversation will help to explain . . .

I looked up after the church service; she was standing near the back. I'd known her since she was Mary in the nativity, since the summers she spent teaching Bible stories at camp. She was a joy. A little girl was letting go of her hand, skipping away to find cookies; an older lady leaned in with sparkling eyes, a smile and "thank you" before slipping out the back. As I approached with, "How are you?" her eyes brimmed with tears. We embraced, and she replied with, "I'm awful, Heather, I'm just terrible." This looked serious. I mentally ditched the afternoon plans. Perhaps Adrian could get a lift home with a friend while I helped this precious one find a way through her calamity. Leading her away from the hubbub of the coffee counter, we found a quieter spot. "I am so sorry for whatever has happened—are you okay?" Her green eyes filled with pain. "All the time, I'm wrong. Every minute of every day. There's never a second when I am not sinning, when I'm not letting God down." I looked at her misery, at the little dancing girl behind her.

What was it that convinced her to shroud her life with God in gloom, to separate a mental belief in His kindness from the delights in her days? And how long before the pirouetting child behind her would learn that she, too, should be despised for her sin and no longer twirl? The disconnection disturbed me—her confession jarred with the beauty around us.

What happens when joy at the love of God is replaced by a brooding self-examination? When we deeply embrace the label of "sinner" and forget the awakening to "saint"? When we recoil from the wonder of divine friendship and replace it with unease?

Theologian Graham Scroggie assigned a title to Psalm 7 that may cause some flinching in church. The heading given in the late nineteenth-century commentary reads, "Psalm 7—NOT GUILTY."[2] He even used caps! How can he endorse David's claim with such confidence? Doesn't the narrative play better when we're altogether wicked, and God is altogether righteous; that even when we do right, we are wrong? It's simpler, cleaner, far less complex.

But that is not what David writes. He says that on this one, he stands blameless. What's more, he writes his claim into a tune and adds harps, lyres, and drums! He does not whine; he doesn't taunt. He doesn't pour hatred down on himself with "I sin all the time and deserve all that's coming."

David studies the accusations hurled against him, with his eternal Friend—violence against the innocent, evil against friends, looting without cause. The conversation is vulnerable, it's honest. In this place of trust, he invites God's judgment to fall on his head if he's lying. He even puts death on the table. It's raw.

David concludes that if God doesn't stand with him against these charges, He's denying His very character. You can almost hear Wesley's "Bold I approach the eternal throne"[3] playing in the background—what an extraordinary bond.

And I'm reminded of a similar scene. One where a man had occasion to crumble, but took steps to do something brave.

Each concert took ages to put together. Grant led the team through months of coffee meetings, planning, and furrowed brows, and then practice, practice, sleep, repeat. On the night of the event, crowds surged in, dividing along dimly lit rows, eyes reflecting the glittered stage. Grant had spotted his mentor in the audience just as the timpani rolled the "Amens." At the end, the audience rose with joy, were held in spellbound wonder. The next day, after the floors were swept and all the instruments tidied away, when nothing more could be done, Grant received the email from his mentor. He clicked the subject line, expecting thanks for the tickets and joy over the event. But the screen widened not to thanks, but to a detailed review. The theme, sound, orchestra, the choice of speaker—the critique dissected each part of the program, expounding on perceived flaws in minute detail. His mentor's intention may have been to support, but the effect was devastation.

Year after year, in the exhaustion of the morning after each concert, the inbox pinged. Spent at the charges brought against him, Grant approached a faithful friend. Could he forward the email, unopened? He no longer had the strength to click. And if there was anything he needed to pay attention to, any place where he'd failed, could his friend let him know so he could address it?

He could have blocked the chiding and sent his mentor's critique to spam, but he brought the accusations to someone he trusted. In all the years of those missives, his friend absorbed the censure and found nothing to condemn. He counted Grant innocent of all the rebuke. In the honest exchange, Grant was at peace.

There is something remarkable taking place in this psalm—the friendship we see is breathtaking. David, in freedom, asks God not just to fight for him, but to establish him, to confirm his virtue in the matter.

The song then develops a mournful note, the tempo drops as the psalmist ponders what's ahead for those who live their life by lies. He anticipates their fall unless they relent. He sees them move beyond the borders of peace. They will dig, and they will fall, and violence will surround. They will face the Almighty's disdain. There's sorrow in the timbre, pity in the chords.

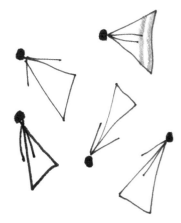

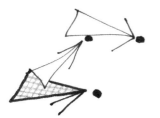

He steps back from the evil and surveys the scene. He is held in the strength of an eternal friendship. Here is safety and strength. He sings out his worship from this place of refuge.

O LORD my God, in You I put my trust;
Save me from all those who persecute me;
And deliver me,
Lest they tear me like a lion,
Rending me in pieces, while there is none to deliver.

PSALM 7, VERSES 1 AND 2

The eleventh-century castle breaking the skyline to the right was quite the distraction in Dr. Scott's history class. We were learning dates and conquests, the victors and the crushed, we didn't look into Napoleon's insecurities or what kept Boudica awake at night. What was recorded for posterity was who left with the loot, who grabbed the most ground.

But people aren't one-dimensional.

The record of you and me may include the odd achievement, but that's the eggshell casing over the whole. For we are textured beings, fragile in our identities and complex in our self-doubt.

The notes heading this lament are "a song sung to the Lord concerning the words of Cush a Benjamite." Not concerning his ninja skills, or his ability to crush bones and slay soldiers, but a song about the words he spoke against the author, about his syllables of threat and accusation. David heard the slander, he was painted as a thief, an ogre, and a tyrant. The whispers were reaching into his friendships, splintering decades of trust. So the unsettled warrior-poet turns to music and begins to grapple with his God.

The opening word addressing the Infinite is "trust." Here is the space where David is seen beyond the headline victories and catastrophic defeats. He is known and believed. All the dimensions of him can come alive. In confidence, assured of welcome, he invites scrutiny from the One who sees.

There is peace in being known beyond the headlines and to be accepted.

DELIVER

O Lord my God in You I put my trust

Save me from all those who persecute me and DELIVER ME

lest they tear me like a lion rending me in pieces while there is none to DELIVER

O Lord my God in You I put my trust

Save me from those who persecute me and DELIVER ME lest they tear

O Lord my God, if I have done this; if there is iniquity in my hands if I have repaid evil to him who was at peace with me or have plundered my enemy without a cause, let the enemy pursue me and overtake me; yes let him trample my life to the earth and lay my honour in the dust. Selah.

O LORD MY GOD I HAVE DONE

O LORD my God, if I have done this:
If there is iniquity in my hands,
If I have repaid evil to him who was at peace with me,
Or have plundered my enemy without cause,
Let the enemy pursue me and overtake me;
Yes, let him trample my life to the earth,
And lay my honor in the dust.
Selah

PSALM 7, VERSES 3 TO 5

Okay, full disclosure, I may have been watching Star Wars the night before this meditation! In the opening of the film, yellow scrolling text about a small band of people trying to bring harmony to the universe "a long time ago in a galaxy far, far away" inadvertently made its way into the image! The conflict between good and evil, between the olive branch of peace and enemies in pursuit tied with this psalm in some corner of my mind. I just saw the connection. Our brains are funny.

Verses 3 to 5 wrestle with lies that have dishonored David's name. He's been accused of raiding without reason and of bringing war on friends, he stands accused of war crimes. But he met his allies in friendship and peace. The slander is disorientating, entirely unfair. It's hateful, it's abhorrent.

Lies are. They are wind in the minds of those who were close; they lift friends out of our reach. We can't cage the gale or make it stop blowing.

The storm of this deception wrecks David.

Selah.

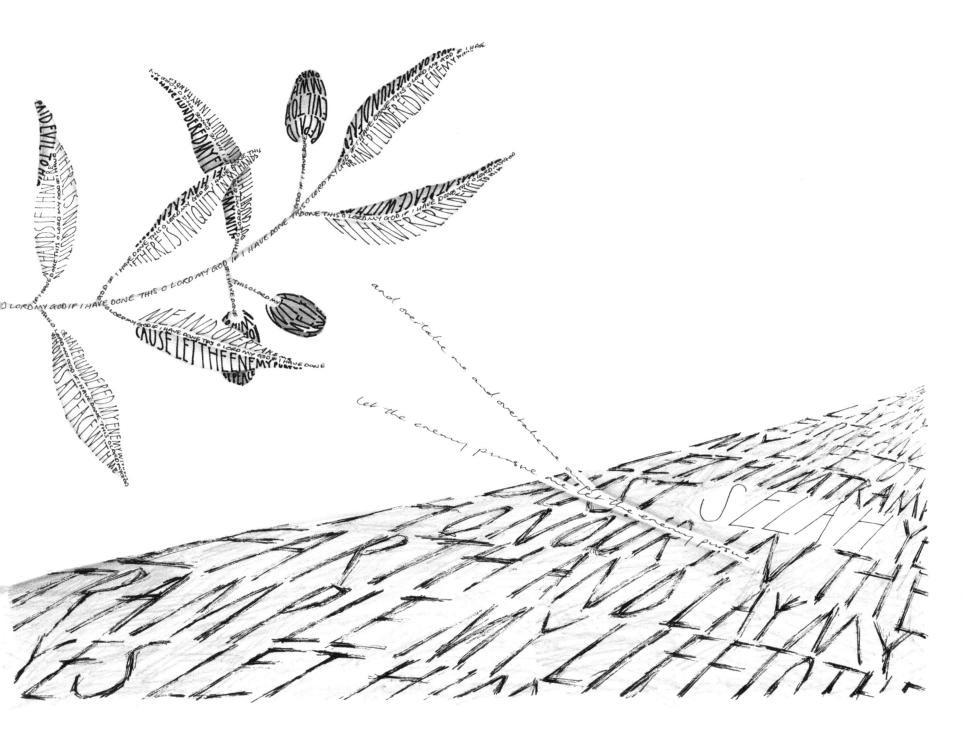

Package deal

Arise, O LORD, in Your anger;
Lift Yourself up because of the rage of my enemies;
Rise up for me to the judgment You have commanded!
So the congregation of the peoples shall surround You;
For their sakes, therefore, return on high.

PSALM 7, VERSES 6 AND 7

The poet has inspected the cogs and wheels of his soul. He finds nothing that has sparked the trouble he's in; there's no cause he can see for the carnage. And his conclusion? *The circumstance is uncalled for. There should be favor. The Almighty has dropped the ball!*

In this ancient text, with tension circling, the writer calls God to stand up and get cross. He takes a look at God's bio, which claims justice in judgment, and gets angry that God's not meeting His resumé. *Step up! Open Your eyes. Implement Your standards, Your own moral code!* is effectively what David calls for. *And do it now.*

It is interesting that he doesn't clean it up. He doesn't temper his anger or move to resignation. He remains in dialogue with God through the heat of it; he doesn't drop his gaze. This passionate relationship is a package deal. There is joy and there is anger, ecstasy and alienation. David meets the Almighty in every emotion and holds it there.

As I drew the words of this verse, I felt the strength of trust between the poet and his God. Although David sees no action, despite the agony of delay, he is relentlessly present.

And they wait. Together.

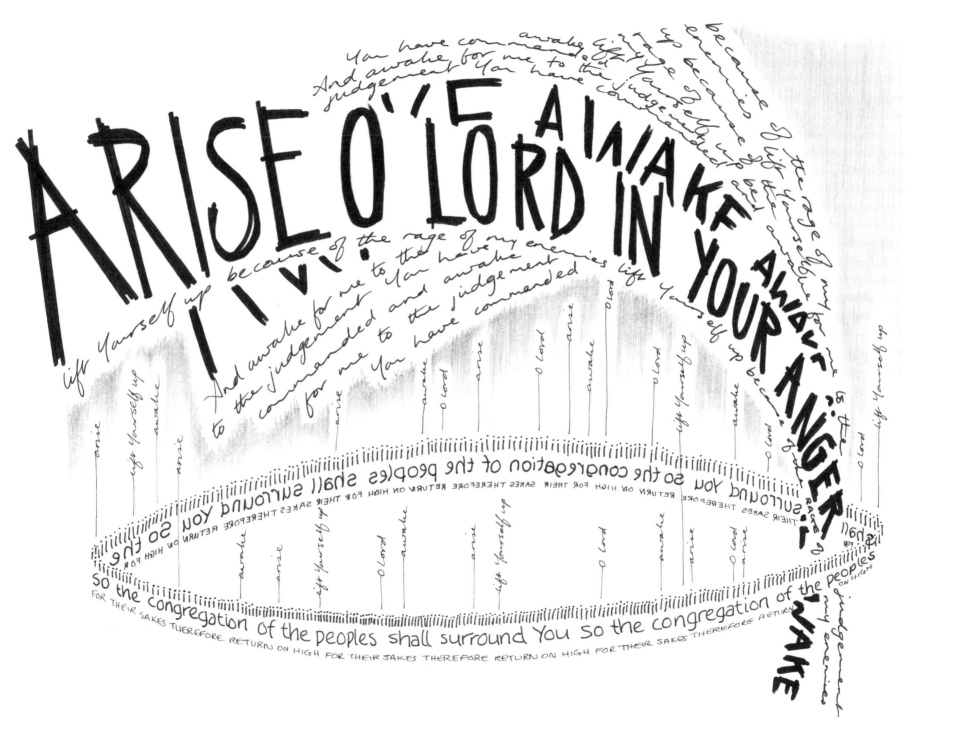

Gutsy move

The LORD shall judge the peoples;
Judge me, O LORD, according to my righteousness,
And according to my integrity within me.
Oh, let the wickedness of the wicked come to an end,
But establish the just;
For the righteous God tests the hearts and minds.
My defense is of God,
Who saves the upright in heart.

PSALM 7, VERSES 8 TO 10

When we hear the word "judgment," linked with an Almighty power, an image of lightning bolts flashes through our minds; and here it formed in this drawing, splitting the page.

From 1000 BC, the psalmist stretches out the scene: A day will come when all will be known, when people will be measured—the secrets they keep, the plans of their hearts. There'll be a day when souls are weighed.

And with this declaration, he takes a brave step. He invites the Almighty to turn the torchlight on *him*, to analyze his story. It's a bold move. *Shine Your light over here. Consider my movements, inspect my heart; look at me God, take Your time. I'm wide open.* What I love here is that David's not squirming around like a grub in the dirt, pleading to be heard. He's standing tall. He didn't do it! The accusations they're flinging at him are the spiked delusions of their sick minds. On this one, he stands upright; he's clean.

And in the turmoil, he asks for a good deal of smiting and doesn't exclude himself from the blitz. With his inner compass whirling and his stomach like the sea, he begs for the evil to stop and cries, *Oh, God, please!* It's an ache.

In a second request, to counter his confusion, he prays, "O LORD . . . establish the just."

We sense his cry. And it's implied in the middle of this terrible storm, *Lord, establish me. Ground me. Plant me secure amidst these acres of evil. Let me stand tall, strengthened by Your verity, watered by Your steadiness, nurtured by Your companionship.*

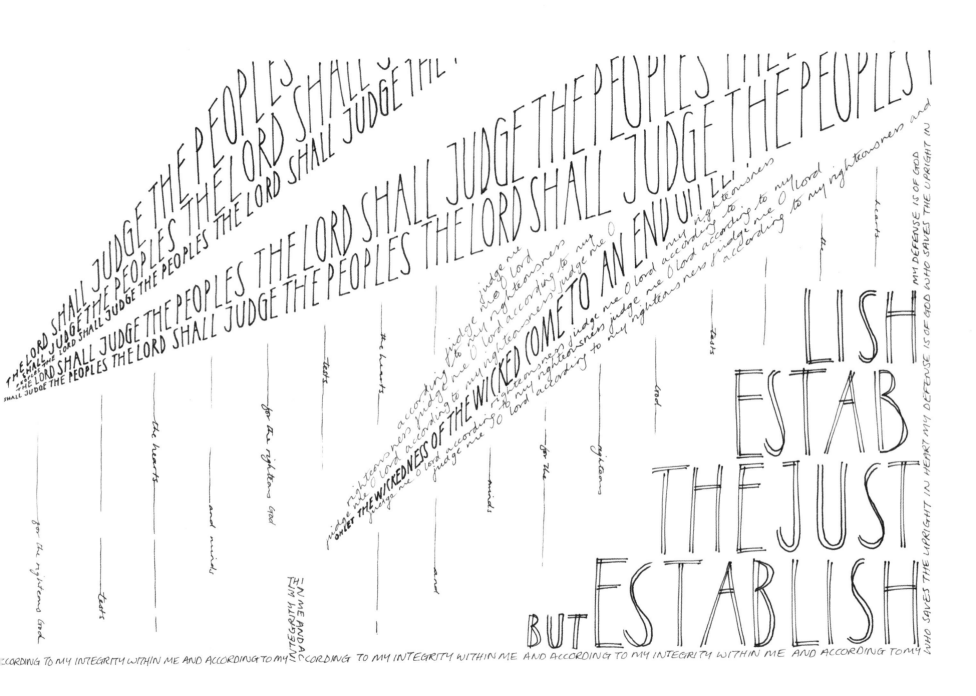

Sleeping in stairwells

God is a just judge,
And God is angry with the wicked every day.
If he does not turn back,
He will sharpen His sword;
He bends His bow and makes it ready.
He also prepares for Himself instruments of death.
He makes His arrows into fiery shafts.

PSALM 7, VERSES 11 TO 13

The words of these verses seem barbaric, even crude. We may be tempted to overlook the poet's sentiment and dismiss it as meant for earlier times. (Surely we're past this sort of primitive behavior; our world has grown up from its savage ways.)

Geography can make us blind.

I received a message a short while back from Lebanon. From bruised and scarred Lebanon where those stretched beyond sense go to buy bread for their children and find their savings have vanished; where resources of food, shelter, and water have run desperately low; where Syrian refugees have swelled the population by 25 percent.

I heard that, in a gathering of anguished believers, a phone had pinged with the image from earlier in this book—"LORD, how they have increased who trouble me! Many are they who rise up against me. Many are they who say of me, 'There is no help for him in God.' But You, O LORD, are a shield for me. My glory and the One who lifts up my head" (Psalm 3:1–3). The phone was passed among those who were fading from hope. And God gave them courage in their gloom.

It was with these brokenhearted people on my mind—mothers choosing which children to feed, families sleeping in stairwells—that I drew the image for these vengeance-laden verses.

God watches the paths of the wicked; He maps out their demise. The words David writes are earthy and dark, but they're also verses of hope. Knowing that God is stirred by evil is stabilizing.

For aching parents huddled in dark stairwells with frightened children pressing in, these are verses of promise. All is seen. There will be justice.

Poetic justice

Behold, the wicked brings forth iniquity;
conceives trouble and brings forth falsehood.
He made a pit and dug it out,
And has fallen into the ditch which he made.
His trouble shall return upon his own head,
And his violent dealing shall come down on his
own crown.

PSALM 7, VERSES 14 TO 16

It's the most satisfying of films that twist at the end. Where headstrong villains who've terrorized the weak are unmasked as small-minded, power hungry, and vain. Best of all is when those who've painstakingly plotted the demise of their rivals fall by their own hand into their own traps!

It's Goliath on the battlefield all over again. The jeering giant threatens to feed David's flesh to the birds . . . and hours later, Goliath's head lies forgotten in the dust. Grim but poetic justice.

These verses lay out the surprise retribution—schemes to trap others for power or pleasure are certain routes to wreckage.[4] The wicked, he writes, will fall by their plots; they'll be snared by their evil designs. The traps they elaborately set for their gain will end up becoming their ruin.

In pride they destroy themselves, while the humble will walk along pavements of gold.

Here is hope for the hounded, justice for the oppressed.

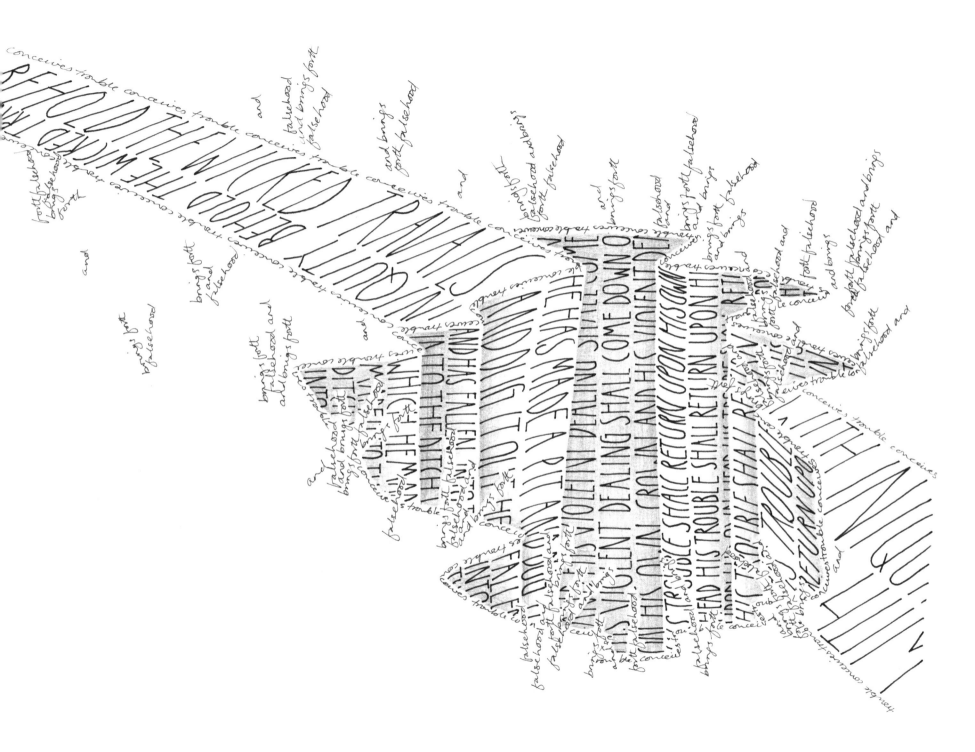

I will praise the LORD according to His righteousness,
And will sing praise to the name of the LORD Most High.

PSALM 7, VERSE 17

At times, we hear that those we run to for help hand out punishments that don't fit the crimes. Our anger rises at disproportionate sanctions. Without fairness, where is our peace?

What if *we're* thrown into jail for walking down the wrong road; what if running a red light is deemed worthy of death? How do we live if we can't trust the protectors . . . what if they misuse their power over *us*?

The basis of the writer's astonished praise is in the character of the Eternal. His integrity has the psalmist singing. God holds all power and sees all evil—from that place of command you'd expect a great deal of smiting of any who dare to do wrong. But the Almighty is not a despot seeking slaves; He lets people's choices run their course, the wicked as well as the good.

And when evil crashes around those who are vile, when horrors fall squarely upon them—this somehow sits right. There is fairness and restraint in the justice of it. God could have used His power to inflict something ghastly, but instead He lets the wicked choose how they will fall.

And David sings—there's safety around a God who is fair, around a King who's entirely righteous.

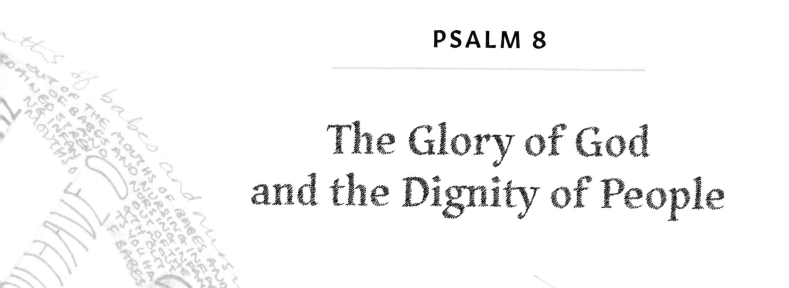

The Glory of God
and the Dignity of People

We've trekked with the fugitive through shadowed valleys where anguish has echoed down forgotten ravines. We've borne his loss of palace and kingdom, felt his ache to be restored to family and home. David lies under skins in desert creeks, yet he is a king, a chariot-rider.

His face has been set on "Zion," Jerusalem, tracing the hill in Psalm 3, prayers from the temple courts in Psalm 4, the threshold of the house of God in Psalm 5, as he steadily moves in closer. The editors of the Psalter have arranged the poems to show us his advance toward the temple and God. Psalms 3 to 7 have asked a lot of us—five strong laments filled with churning emotion, stirred up anguish and desert dust. "The wicked" have condemned, defiled, and stolen his name. As the imagery becomes stronger, the taunts increasingly vile, we come upon this stunning song.

Psalm 8 has an altogether different texture from what has come before. David sings of someone greater than all who warred against him, someone mightier than their strongholds and wealthier than their kings. The turmoil we've come through subsides, and we can draw our breath. We lean in to an exchange between a warrior and his God—and it's not a strategy meeting about villains, nor a plan to exploit his foes. What we hear in this "short exquisite lyric"[1] is wonder.

David is overcome with the magnitude of creation—the evening's molten skies pour their gold over the landscape, and shadows slowly blot the light from faces, animals, and fields. The universe then puts on her breathless display, moon and stars emerge from the blackening beauty as the earth is cloaked in awe.

He's no longer dazed by the battle nor crushed by lament. He is transported to the truest dimension of his being and sees more.

Naturalist William Beebe wrote of an evening ritual between himself and Theodore Roosevelt. Beebe writes:

Theodore Roosevelt and I, after an evening of talk, would go out on the lawn and search the skies until we found the faint spot of light-mist beyond the lower left-hand corner of the Great Square of Pegasus. Then one or the other of us would recite: "That is the spiral galaxy in Andromeda. It is as large as our Milky Way. It is one of a hundred million galaxies. It consists of one hundred billion suns, each larger than our sun." Then Roosevelt would grin at me and say, "Now I think we are small enough. Let's go to bed."[2]

While the world ripped itself apart during the Second World War, while all around families ached for peace, these men, like the psalmist, turned their gaze to the heavens and rested in the smallness of their greatness.

David takes it further and writes of things that lie behind the world that we can see—the dawning of time, the thoughts on God's mind. He sings with wonder of a lopsided friendship between a creature and his Creator, between a chariot-rider and the Maker of the earth on which he rides.

Are we now to join in harmonies and thunderous Amens, raise our crescendos and shout with joy? Unusually for a psalm of praise, David invites no one into his song. He stands alone in Psalm 8, a tiny being before his God, astonished at the Almighty's condescension—that uncontainable power would stoop so low, that humanity's weakness could be transformed into strength, that babbling praise could silence the strong.

He continues in wonder and unstoppable praise—singing of angels, of God's love for people, and that despite their angst and "disordered loves"[3] their Maker draws them close. David sings that he's accepted, robed with glory and honor; a coronation has taken place before the throne of God. But what of his kingdom, his hardship and exile? They no longer consume his mind. David stands in a kingdom where God reigns supreme. Humanity isn't the afterthought of day six of creation, each one is invited into the most hallowed of friendships. Emerson writes, "All I have seen teaches me to trust the Creator for all I have not seen."[4] David stands in a kingdom where God reigns.

He closes with the words from the start of the song, that Yahweh the covenant keeper, that Adonai his master reigns above all the boundaries of earth. Even the heavens cannot hold Him.

And he is at rest. The King of heaven, his *Friend*, has brought him near.

African skies

O LORD, our Lord,
How excellent is Your name in all the earth,
You who set Your glory above the heavens!

PSALM 8, VERSE 1

For the first eleven years of my life, I lived just outside the beautiful city of Cape Town, where chameleons and tortoises wandered into the garden and bright birds flashed overhead. On some starry nights, in front of the porch, my father would shake out an old tartan blanket, stretching it over the dried up grass. And we'd lie on our backs in the enveloping darkness, gazing into the African sky. I'd forget all about the scratchy wool as my eyes adjusted to the wonder above. Breathtaking constellations crisscrossed the night as we listened to his voice and followed his pointing finger.

But somehow I caught the story wrong. For years I thought stars were holes in the sky, pinpricks in the canopy. I thought they were flecks of light that blinked through the cover, and behind it, oh, behind it was light and the shining beauty of heaven!

And learning of solar systems, planets, and galaxies, I've still not shaken that wonder—that as we look up, we see the tiniest fraction of what is beyond.

Here David sings as he stares into the sky, that *the* Lord is *our* Lord. That the splendor and mystery of Him sits above all our dreaming!

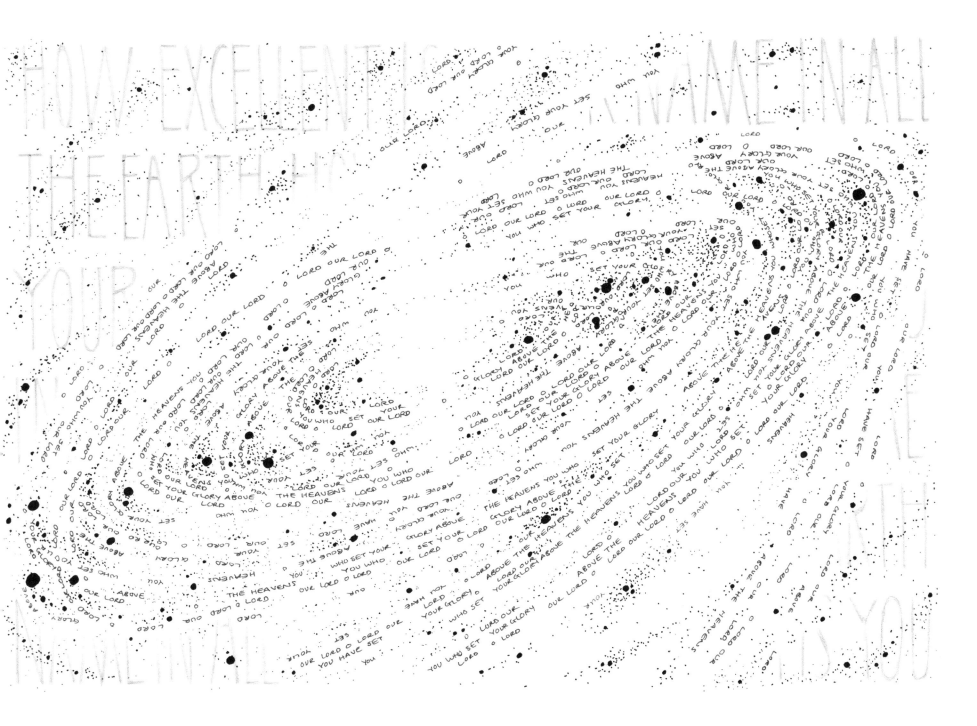

Soft skin

Out of the mouth of babes and nursing infants
You have ordained strength,
Because of Your enemies,
That You may silence the enemy and the avenger.

PSALM 8, VERSE 2

This verse is a puzzle. It doesn't make sense—how does a baby show strength or give God praise? On their best days, they gurgle and give gummy smiles; they're characteristically cute, not impressive!

Yet David says it is *babies* who silence his foes ... but how?

The clue to the answer is a few verses on where the poet talks to God about the worth of a man. "You have *made* him a little lower than the angels, and You have crowned him with glory and honor" (verse 5). It is at the *making* stage that we're crowned with glory and given esteem. When God knits molecules and atoms, noses and toes, when He assembles our souls—*that* is the point we are crowned.

Infants testify to God's mastery and design before they speak a syllable or lift a mic. David says the transcendence of God is shown in the very fact that babies are here, that they've been built to breathe and to be. The Almighty displays His strength in the powerless—it's the theme that infuses the whole of the sacred text.

And it matches the way that He spoke of His Son—it was before the lad from Nazareth had done anything more than fix plows and mend tables that His Father said He was beloved, that He took delight in Him.[5]

God's very act of creation is the silencer. It undoes defenses. His genius is clothed in weakness, His strength in soft skin.

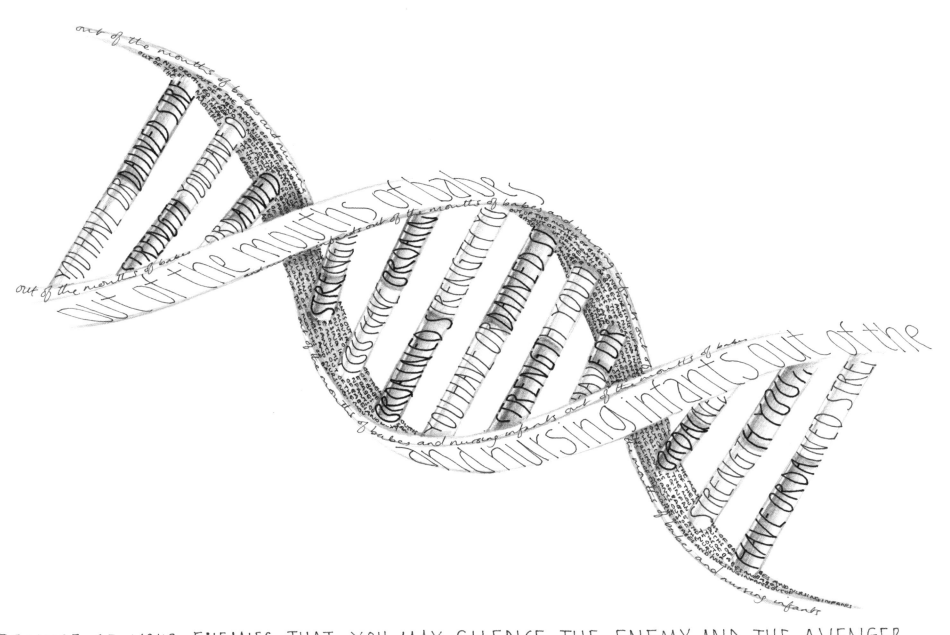

BECAUSE OF YOUR ENEMIES THAT YOU MAY SILENCE THE ENEMY AND THE AVENGER.

Lamplight and stars

When I consider Your heavens, the work of Your fingers,
The moon and the stars, which You have ordained,
What is man that You are mindful of him,
And the son of man that You visit him?
For You have made him a little lower than the angels,
And You have crowned him with glory and honor.

PSALM 8, VERSES 3 TO 5

This prayer was likely breathed in David's closing years.[6] A lifetime of adventure swells beneath each phrase.

I imagine the lamplight with the old king looking up from his papyrus to the canopy of the heavens, gazing in wonder as stars infuse the empty space. He is silent before splendor, awed by the majesty, and utterly bewildered that the Creator of all this has tended him.

This translation of the psalm left the fourth line as, "You visit him." In many translations, the words chosen are "You care for him."[7] (Both have me smiling, but I find my eyes are crinkling at "visit.") It's care in action. It's leaving your home to come to mine. It's effort, movement, presence.

And David, the sovereign, is overwhelmed by it. His song becomes unrestrained worship. The joy of this communion is a far greater glory than all the gold in his kingdom or the crown on his head.

Here is peace.

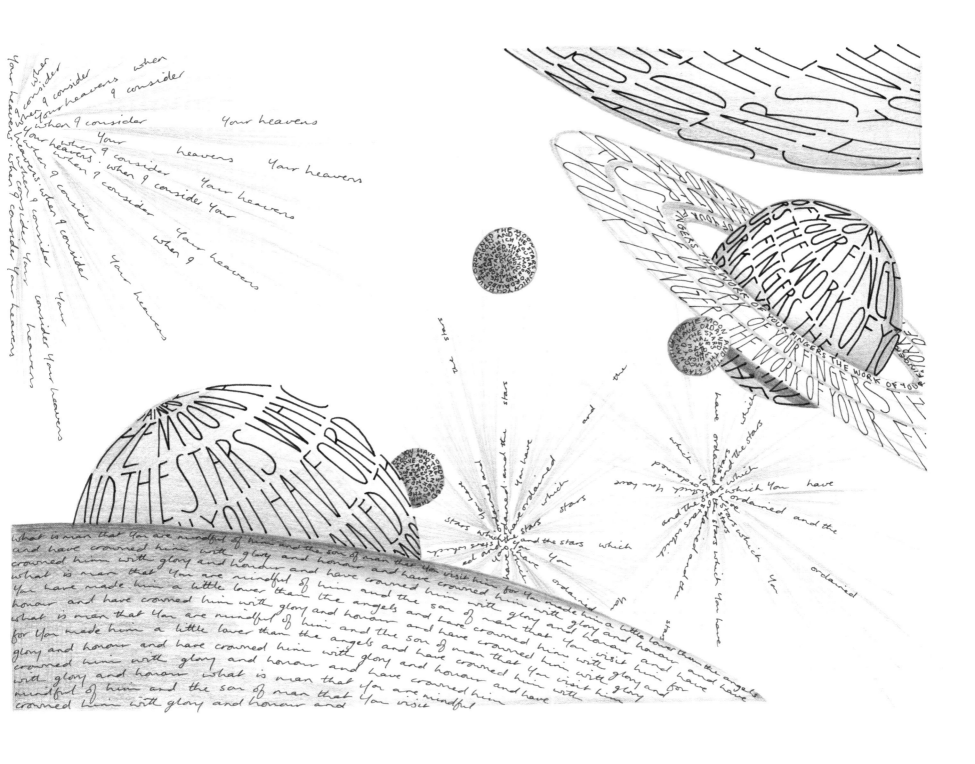

Birds and beasts

You have made him to have dominion over the works
of Your hands;
You have put all things under his feet,
All sheep and oxen—
Even the beasts of the field,
The birds of the air,
And the fish of the sea
That pass through the paths of the seas.

PSALM 8, VERSES 6 TO 8

From the wonder of sparkling skies, we extend our gaze to the glow of the morning, and we arrive in Eden. The poem vibrates with the crystalline days of the creation narrative. Where light sparkles on unsullied lakes, as giraffes and llamas, anteaters and cubs, emerge from a dew-laden undergrowth. And we hear the voice of Adam, fresh from the hand of Omnipotence.

The guardianship of God's creation masterpiece wasn't some spontaneous idea at the end of a day of sharing the sights—wildebeest flowing across the plains and whales cresting on the horizon would put anyone in a great mood, ready to share their treasures. No, God's intention all along was to commission Adam to tend His dazzling work.

The day started with a dust creature breathing in life, and ended with him being appointed to care for all that he saw. What a promotion!

You have made him to have dominion over the works of Your hands
You have put all things under his feet

THE BIRDS OF THE AIR THE BIRDS

OF THE AIR THE BIRDS OF THE AIR THE

EVEN THE BEASTS OF THE FIELD EVEN THE BEASTS OF THE FIELD EVEN THE

SHEEP

OXEN

ALL ALL ALL

AND AND AND AND AND

EVEN THE BEASTS OF THE FIELD EVEN THE

EVEN THE BEASTS OF THE FIELD EVEN THE

AND THE

FISH OF THE SEA

THAT PASS THROUGH

THE PATHS OF THE SEA AND THE FISH OF THE

SEA THAT PASS

Thumping tables

O LORD, our Lord,
How excellent is Your name in all the earth!

PSALM 8, VERSE 9

Last night, sheet lightning lit up our sky. Thunder rolled through the streets to the shaking horizon. We went to sleep with its rumbling and woke to distant echoes with the dawn (I left the curtains open to watch and to tremble!). You can't shut out the thunder.

The eighth psalm has looked at each dimension of living. From tiny children to those at war, from docile animals to untamed beasts, the teeming seas, the crowded air, the splendor of the universe—in every space David looks for someone more majestic, more precious, and more dear.

And his conclusion? In all the earth there are rumbles of God, echoing His beauty. He cannot be shut out!

In my mind, the old king is thumping the table, standing up, shouting out what he's found: "'O LORD, our Lord, How excellent is Your name in all the earth.'"

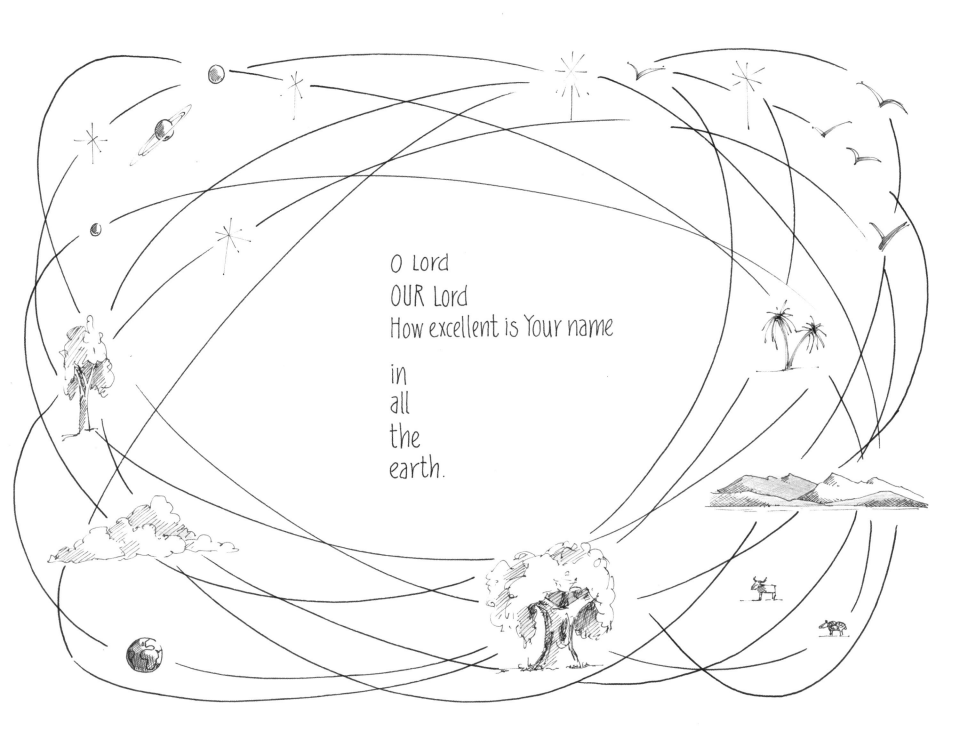

O Lord
OUR Lord
How excellent is Your name

in
all
the
earth.

Prayer of Thanks for Justice—
A Lament of David

Confidence is armor—when we wear it, we shine. The songwriter gleams! He is secure in his claims. He positions each one into an acrostic poem through Psalms 9 and 10. He fills verses with verbs, holding nothing back—*I will praise, tell, rejoice, sing, and … for your information … my enemies will fall*.[1] Courage flashes through the blue sky like so many glinting arrows fired from his stronghold.

Here we find out something crucial about David: his being is wrapped up in God. Each direction he faces, every path he treads, the King of heaven fills his sight. There's very little of Psalm 9 that's directed *to* God, as David can't stop telling everyone *about* Him! His excitement is contagious. Excitement is! When we're amazed at what we've found, our news spreads.

Last week, our friends tried the new Italian restaurant in town. For days, all we heard about was the thinness of the crust, the melt-in-the-mouth mozzarella, the incredible tiramisu! They couldn't contain how fabulous it was; they kept going back to the wonder. Over and over, "But did we tell you about the crust?" "Yes, four times already!" We laughed together at their evangelistic zeal.

David's uninhibited joy at what he has found fills the pages. He keeps uncovering more reasons to praise.

The focus then shifts to expansive pronouncements of powerful end-of-days stuff. We haven't heard this since Psalm 2 at the start of the Psalter—there's justice and rule, thrones and judgment, destruction and eternal vanishing—it's apocalyptic! The "blotting out" and "destroying" haven't taken place yet, but the psalmist writes as if it's all over. He records it in the past tense. What's going on?

David's certainty goes beyond what he can see, for he knows the nature of the One who lives in his future. He's not projecting good vibes to impact what's coming; this isn't magical thinking. David is as sure of what will happen as night follows day. He knows who God is, so he knows what is coming, it makes sense that he pens it as "done." David sings out a level of certainty that's astonishing and writes it all in the past tense.

A missionary friend came to church after a decade overseas. During one Sunday service, Matt told us about the people he served and the dangers that they faced. As he spoke of his distress, pain pushed down on his brows, compassion spilled over his cheeks. "Please could you pray that the fighting would stop, that families would grow up with fathers?" He left the stage to the chords of an upbeat praise song, his sadness jarred with the happy program. As the tune ended, the adults settled in for the sermon, and the children ran excitedly to the Sunday school door. Matt went with them to speak in their classes, to answer their questions and ask for their prayers.

When he finished showing photos and writing prayer points on the board, a small hand shot up, asking, "Please can I pray?" With the teacher's nod, little Josh stood up from where he'd been sitting, cross-legged on the floor. He scratched his head, blond hair tousled, then earnestly began to pray "Thank You God that You will . . ." He started each request with the same line. The eight-year-old boy laid out the expectations he had of his heavenly Friend. He led each request with gratitude; he *began* with belief. That

these things hadn't happened yet was an insignificant detail in his vibrant faith. The One he turned to was listening and strong, so he brought it all without hesitation to God.

Where do we turn as we move through the hubbub of our years, for there's a thousand voices shaping who we become? We may rely on a celebrity or a spouse to form our values, a sports team or church to govern our thoughts; or perhaps we pick a preacher to follow, to keep things on the right track. The challenge with all these objects of worship is that they drift. Like Sahara sands they peak and trough. All it takes is one storm for the landscape to change.

David's song, and whole life, hang on verse 10 of this psalm: "Those who know Your name will put their trust in You." There is something about knowledge of the character of God that awakens confidence in us and stirs a steadying hope. For "few delights can equal the mere presence of one whom we trust utterly."[2] Trust between a mortal and the Infinite is the strength of life, holding our uncertainties and joys together. We don't need an inconsistent God, shifting like the desert floor. The One we rely on must be as secure as Everest. He needs to be rock-like, safe, solid. (Does this sound a bit dull? These aren't words to inspire.) But this song is anything but boring! It's filled with adventure, not duty and gloom.

I remember the first time I heard that God doesn't change. I crowded in with a dozen children to sit cross-legged on the rug, grateful to be out of the African sun and happy that this Bible club teacher didn't insist we wear shoes. She beamed down, announcing the main point of her story: God never changes. We even had a song about it. I was thrown. "Unchanging" felt dreary, like cold stone pulpits above dusty pews, dismal sermons with threadbare hymnbooks. God sounded like a faded yesterday, who had little to offer my colorful world. I filed the thought in a stack of forgettable things.

The strategy worked splendidly until twenty-five years later when a seminary professor asked us to depict, in visual form, the attributes of God. Now, I love a creative assignment! Finding a palette, I began painting the colors of grace, love, sovereignty, truth; but then I came across the one I'd stored away so many years before. The image from that barefoot classroom resurfaced. There must be more to "unchanging" than being out-of-date? It didn't match the vibrant friendship I enjoyed with the Lord. Drab and predictable didn't come into it!

Perhaps the translators had had an off day. They'd missed a *yod* or a *tav*, were distracted by a chirping cricket and accidentally wrote that God is unchanging, rather than He is exciting!

I wrestled with the word until one description rang true. Lifting the palette knife, reds and yellows burned across the canvas. I painted fire. Fire: unchanging in its elements and uncontainable in its reach. Yes, this was it; here is what I experienced of this remarkable Redeemer. I beamed as I looked at the glimpse of God I had painted: steadfastly radiant, consistently immense. The sight of it stretched out praise in my soul.

As maids and princesses, farmers and kings meet God through the Bible narratives, they name what they see. When He steps into their pain and their joys, we find hints of who He is. But their God is our God—so when demands overwhelm, and we've run out of hope, *we* can lean in to El Shaddai, the all-sufficient One. When overlooked and disregarded, we turn to El Roi, the God who sees. When terror surrounds and there isn't a way to quiet our soul, we rest in Jehovah Shalom, our peace. When the valley is shadowed and darkness encroaches, Jehovah Raah is our Shepherd. When we never imagined drifting this far and goodness seems a decade away, Jehovah Shammah, the Lord is there.

And David got it. He wrote it loud in this song, singing out of a life of hope. "Those who know Your name will put their trust in You."

"You are incredible"

I will praise You, O LORD, with my whole heart;
I will tell of all Your marvelous works.
I will be glad and rejoice in You;
I will sing praise to Your name, O Most High.

PSALM 9, VERSES 1 AND 2

"I find it difficult to praise," said a confident student in an unguarded moment, "or to be grateful." I sat awhile with the statement, grateful for his vulnerability, considering the predicament.

What stops us praising, what holds us back, what stifles our joy at others' success? For this ancient writing is effusive, a barrage of joy bursting into applause!

It was during the Covid-19 pandemic when we drove past the huge billboard. They're mostly visually noisy things filled with faces and slogans and pressure to buy, but this one was still. One color, two lines: "Thank you to our care workers. You are incredible," with the small insignia of the Scottish Parliament beneath. I choked up with gratitude, spilled over with praise.

Through months of lockdown, billions of people had been cemented together by one unifying fear: we cannot fix this no matter how lovely or powerful we are. We do not contribute to the cure. All the healing lies in the hands of others as they risk their lives to save ours. Praise and naked "thank yous" burst from our souls and drop from our eyes.

I think that's what David saw. He wasn't enough for the situation he faced; it was vast, paralyzing. But in strength and with healing, Love stepped in and held him steady. So he ditched all decorum and burst into praise.

Wholehearted thanksgiving comes when we realize we're not enough, He is. And He's all in.

I will be glad and rejoice in You I will be glad and rejoice in

I will tell of all your marvellous works

I will sing praise to Your name O Most High O Most High

I will be glad and rejoice in You

IN YOU IN YOU YOU

O MOST HIGH O MOST

I will praise you O Lord with my whole O Most High O

I will be glad and rejoice

O MOST HIGH

praise to You

You O Lord with my

I will tell of all Your

and rejoice in You I will sing praise to Your

HIGH O MOST HIGH

I will be glad

with my whole heart

and rejoice in You

I will sing praise to Your name

I will praise You O Lord with my whole heart I will praise You O Lord

I will sing praise

I will sing

in You   in You

You O Lord with my

to Your name

LORD WITH MY WHOLE

will praise You O Lord with my whole heart I will praise

I will be glad

WORKS I will tell of all Your marvellous works

You I will be glad and

I will be glad and rejoice in You

I will be glad

I will praise You O Lord

I will be glad and rejoice in You

and rejoice in You

O MOST HIGH O MOST HIGH O MOST HIGH O MOST

I will be glad

I will tell of all Your marvellous works I will be glad

You I will be glad and rejoice in You

MOST HIGH O MOST HIGH IN YOU IN YOU

O MOST HIGH O MOST HIGH

O MOST HIGH

and rejoice in You

I will praise You O Lord with my whole heart I will tell of all Your marvellous works I will praise

I will tell of all Your marvellous works I will tell of all Your marvellous works I will praise

I will praise You O Lord with my whole heart I will praise

O Most High   I will be glad and rejoice in You O Lord

I will praise You O Lord with my whole heart

I will sing praise to Your name I will sing

High O Most High O Most High O Most High O Most High

with my whole heart

with my whole heart

O MOST HIGH

WITH MY WHOLE HEART

The startling statement

When my enemies turn back,
They shall fall and perish at Your presence.
For You have maintained my right and my cause;
You sat on the throne judging in righteousness.

PSALM 9, VERSES 3 AND 4

Bullying at work is a scourge on our spirits, stealing peace from our days and sleep from our nights. We can find ourselves in awkward mediation meetings with someone in authority, who can make it stop. What we need is a leader who calls out bad behavior, but there are bosses who want to be liked, who step back from making a judgment to "keep in" with all involved. They justify their refusal to lead with, "I have to walk a middle road."

Is this what we need in situations of tyranny? A choreographed space between parties where, no matter where truth lies, both can be pleased that they are equidistant from the other? Is symmetry the high point of justice?

These are the last words we want to hear in a conflict.

The objective in a courtroom is not layout; it is truth—no matter how near or far from it, the other side it sits. We need the gavel to fall on the side of true north, for actions to be measured from something that's firm.

David writes that the Almighty is concerned with righteousness, not with composition; that the rules remain the same no matter who's in the dock. He sits with truth. If we are wide of it, we cannot stand; but if truth is what we're holding, we'll find ourselves sitting right next to Him, swinging our legs. At peace. In freedom. Whole.

This is the "still point of the turning world."[3] A place where it's easy to hope.

When my enemies turn back they shall fall and perish at Your presence

When my enemies turn back then shall fall and perish at Your presence

YOU SAT ON THE THRONE JUDGING IN RIGHTEOUSNESS YOU SAT ON THE THRONE

JUDGING IN RIGHTEOUSNESS YOU SAT ON THE THRONE JUDGING IN RIGHT

YOU SAT ON THE THRONE

You have rebuked the nations,
You have destroyed the wicked;
You have blotted out their name forever and ever.

O enemy, destructions are finished forever!
And you have destroyed cities;
Even their memory has perished.

But the LORD shall endure forever;
He has prepared His throne for judgment.
He shall judge the world in righteousness,
And He shall administer judgment for the peoples
in uprightness.

PSALM 9, VERSES 5 TO 8

All of us, spinning on this little blue planet and currently flying through its skies, have our hands on a gift: we receive one life—its length, to be discovered; its direction and drift, largely up to us.

The wicked have used their gift of life to gain power, to grab at others' wealth. It doesn't concern them whose treasures they trample, whose lives they destroy. They build their cities on the ruin of others.

And we sense abhorrence in the heart of the Giver: He speaks to the wicked, but they do not change; chides, but they don't shift. The tension in the text builds—the gifts of life they were given are withdrawn, the cities they commanded are destroyed, their very existence is forgotten. All the evil they inflicted on others is delivered to their door.

Ancient words map the epic scene, the lands that were consumed by their greed hold no memory that they even existed. The throne of the Lord rises above lands that have forgotten their names. The gavel rises with integrity and falls with justice. And no one protests. The rulings are sound.

BUT THE LORD SHALL ENDURE FOREVER

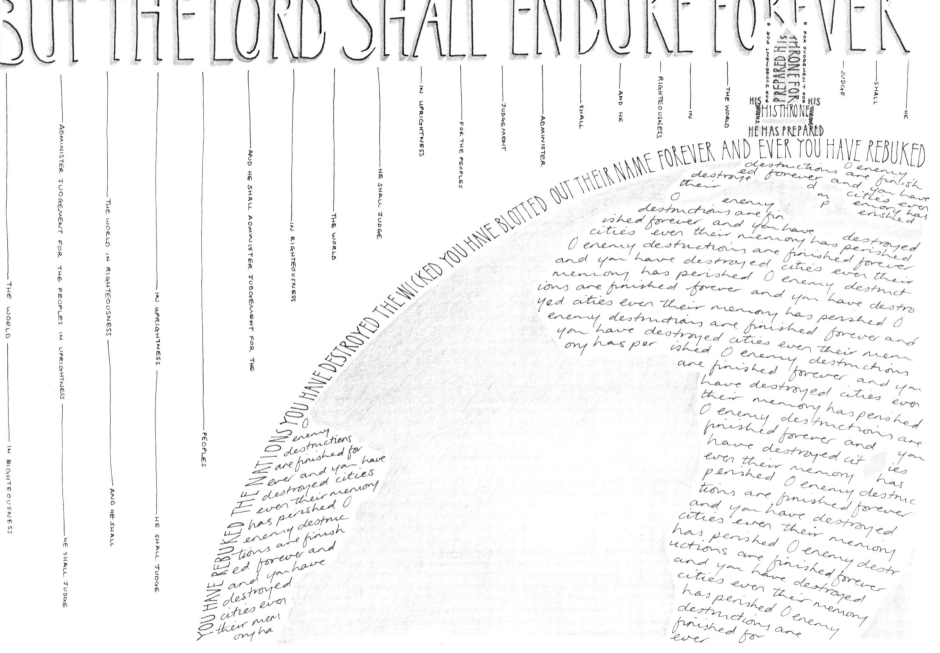

THE WORLD

ADMINISTER JUDGEMENT FOR THE PEOPLES IN UPRIGHTNESS

THE WORLD IN RIGHTEOUSNESS

IN UPRIGHTNESS

AND HE SHALL ADMINISTER JUDGEMENT FOR THE

IN RIGHTEOUSNESS

THE WORLD

HE SHALL JUDGE

FOR THE PEOPLES

JUDGEMENT

ADMINISTER

SHALL

AND HE

RIGHTEOUSNESS

IN

THE WORLD

JUDGE

SHALL

HE

THE WORLD

IN RIGHTEOUSNESS

HE SHALL JUDGE

AND HE SHALL

IN UPRIGHTNESS

HE SHALL JUDGE

PEOPLES

THRONE FOR HIS THRONE
FOR JUDGEMENT FOR HIS
PREPARED
HIS THRONE
HE HAS PREPARED

FOR JUDGEMENT FOR HIS
THRONE FOR HIS

HE HAS PREPARED

FOREVER AND EVER YOU HAVE REBUKED THE NATIONS YOU HAVE DESTROYED THE WICKED YOU HAVE BLOTTED OUT THEIR NAME FOREVER AND EVER YOU HAVE REBUKED

O enemy destructions are finished forever and you have destroyed cities even their memory has perished O enemy destructions are finished forever and you have destroyed cities even their memory has perished O enemy destructions are finished forever and you have destroyed cities even their memory has perished O enemy destructions are finished forever and you have destroyed cities even their memory has perished O enemy destructions are finished forever and you have destroyed cities even their memory has perished O enemy destructions are finished forever and you have destroyed cities even their memory has perished O enemy destructions are finished forever and you have destroyed cities even their memory has perished O enemy destructions are finished forever and you have destroyed cities even their memory has perished O enemy destructions are finished forever

O enemy destructions are finished forever and you have destroyed cities even their memory has perished O enemy destructions are finished forever and you have destroyed cities even their memory has per ished O enemy destructions are finished forever and you have destroyed cities even their memory has perished O enemy destructions are finished forever and you have destroyed cities even their memory has perished O enemy destructions are finished forever and you have destroyed cities even their memory has perished O enemy destructions are finished forever and you have destroyed cities even their memory has perished O enemy destructions are finished forever and you have destroyed cities even their memory has perished O enemy destructions are finished forever

Held

The LORD will be a refuge for the oppressed,
A refuge in times of trouble.
And those who know Your name will put their trust in You;
For You, LORD, have not forsaken those who seek You.

PSALM 9, VERSES 9 AND 10

In oppression, He is refuge. In trouble, there is trust. We are not forsaken.

Today, be held.

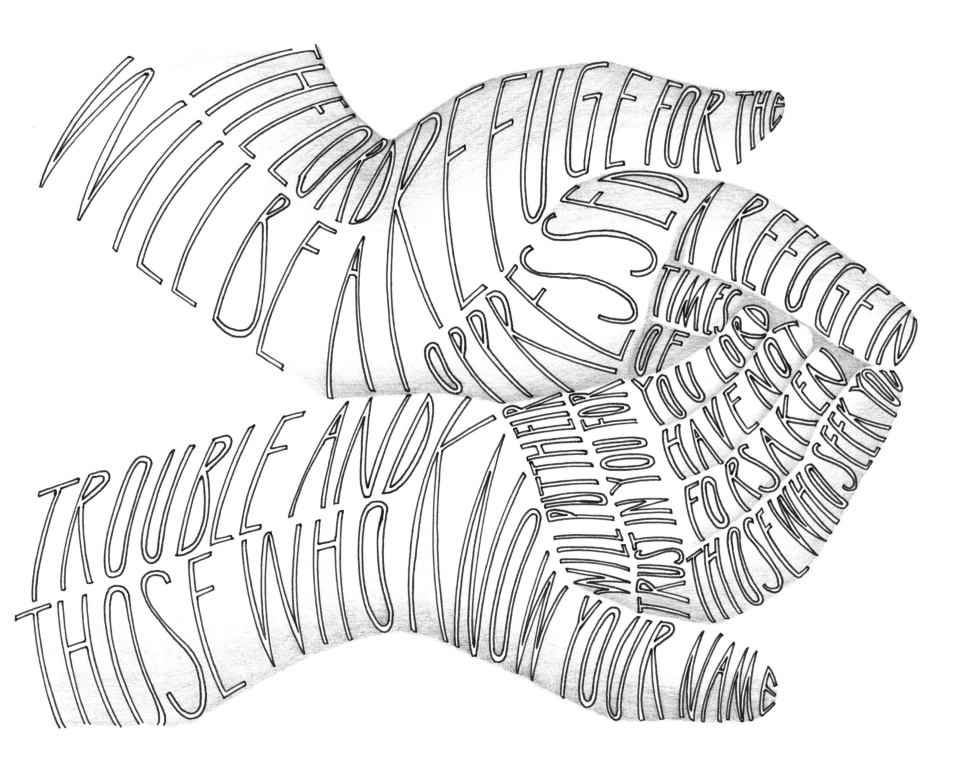

Righting wrongs

Sing praises to the LORD, who dwells in Zion!
Declare His deeds among the people.
When He avenges blood, He remembers them;
He does not forget the cry of the humble.

PSALM 9, VERSES 11 AND 12

I don't remember all my grandparents' names. Not my great-grandparents, but my mum's and dad's mum and dad. We're going through life thinking we're memorable, and right now, maybe we are. There's perhaps a few toes filled in on our digital footprint, a couple of accolades here and there.

But I don't remember my grandparents' *names*. Not their jobs or achievements, but the first thing that was said in handshakes with strangers. Their memory is being erased. It's sobering.

The contrast stuns. What is lodged in the mind of Omniscience, David writes, is not the resumés of the great and the good, but the stifled cries of the weak and the buried cruelty of the strong. And, He assures, it's not "if," it is "when" He brings those abuses to book.

Declare it, sing it out! He does not forget the cry of the humble.

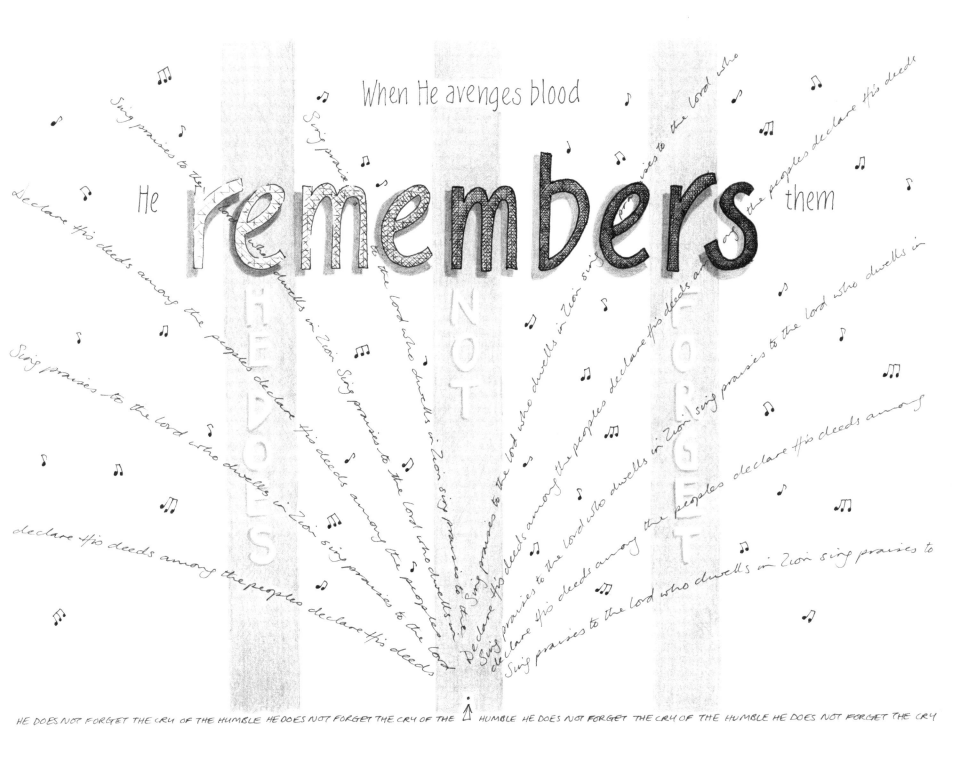

Grim gates

Have mercy on me, O Lord!
Consider my trouble from those who hate me,
You who lift me up from the gates of death,
That I may tell of all Your praise
In the gates of the daughter of Zion.
I will rejoice in Your salvation.

PSALM 9, VERSES 13 AND 14

David wrote songs that carried thanks to the heavens: the Almighty came through in the past. But on this day, hatred is battering at his door.

There is more trouble than he can shrug off. The conflict is deep and cruel. He isn't ready for his voice to be silenced, for his path to come to an end. So David looks up from the borders of life and asks God to study the pain (I've written it tiny in the drawing so that you have to come close).

The poet then speaks of two gates; you can find them in the drawing. Gates were where kings made judgments and where prophets called out insights. Gates were all about vision and future; they were where things got done!

So he pleads for action, for movement. For God to lift him from the place of silence to a wide open door, where he can shout out about rescue, about future and about joy.

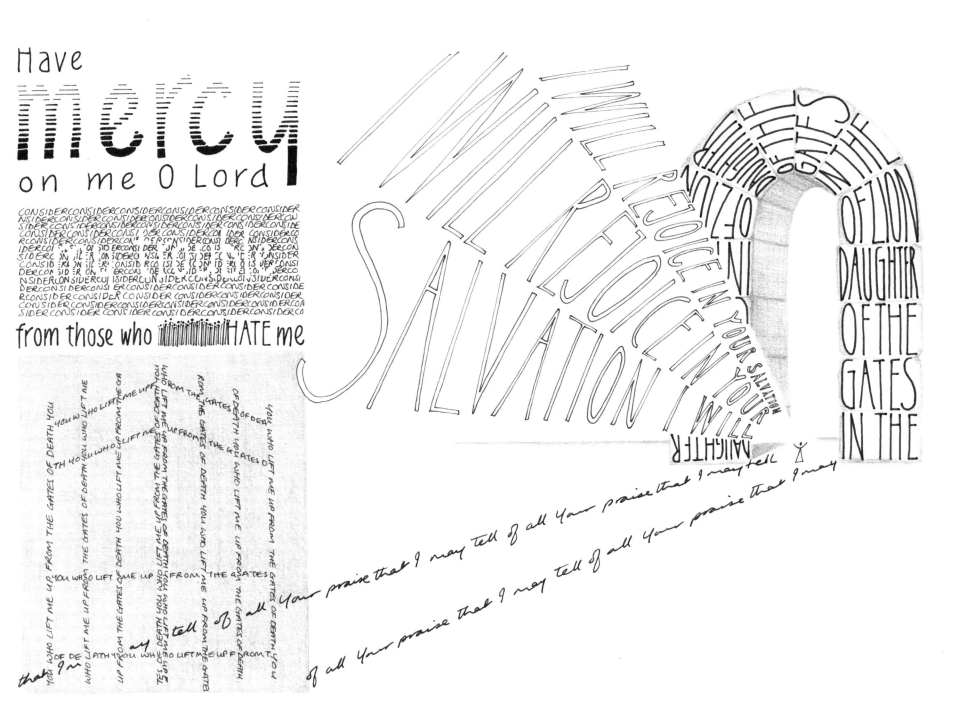

Have mercy on me O Lord

CONSIDER CONSIDER CONSIDER CONSIDER CONSIDER CONSIDER CONSIDER CONSIDER CONSIDER CONSIDER CONSIDER CONSIDER CON SIDER CONSIDER CONSIDER CONSIDER CONSIDER CONSIDER CONSIDER CONSIDER CONSIDER CONSIDER CONSIDER CONSIDER CONSIDER CONSIDER CONSIDER CONSIDER

from those who HATE me

YOU WHO LIFT ME UP FROM THE GATES OF DEATH

I WILL REJOICE IN YOUR SALVATION SALVATION DAUGHTER OF ZION DAUGHTER OF THE GATES

DAUGHTER OF ZION DAUGHTER OF THE GATES IN THE

that I may tell of all Your praise that I may tell of all Your praise that I may tell of all Your praise that I may tell of all Your praise that I may

The nations have sunk down in the pit which they made;
In the net which they hid, their own foot is caught.
The LORD is known by the judgment He executes;
The wicked is snared in the work of his own hands.
Meditation.
Selah

PSALM 9, VERSES 15 AND 16

You can tell Van Gogh by the brushstrokes, Michelangelo by the muscles, Miro by the blue. In classical music, you can spot Beethoven by the forceful rhythm and Bach by the intricate counterpoint. The form of the creation reveals its maker; there's no need to sign the masterpiece.

I wonder if this transfers to a court of law. Can a judge can be identified by the rulings that are given?

There are patterns developing through these laments of anguish, confession, and war, and the Almighty's response to this evil is impressively consistent. Pits are dug to trap the weak, and the one who digs them falls in; nets are stretched to enslave and wound, and the selfish trappers are ensnared.

It's justice on repeat—and deeply satisfying.

But, as the verses lay out, it leads to reflection and a good deal of unease! If this *is* the pattern, if there's consistency across the board, the judgment for them is the judgment for me. And in some dusty corner of my mind, the liturgy rumbles:

> *Almighty and most merciful Father,*
> *we have wandered and strayed*
> *from Your ways like lost sheep.*
> *We have followed too much the devices*
> *and desires of our own hearts.*
> *We have offended against Your holy laws.*
> *We have left undone those things*
> *that we ought to have done;*
> *and we have done those things*
> *that we ought not to have done;*
> *and there is no health in us.*
> *But You, O Lord, have mercy upon us sinners.*
> *Spare those who confess their faults.*
> *Restore those who are penitent,*
> *according to your promises declared*
> *to mankind in Christ Jesus our Lord.*
> *And grant, O most merciful Father, for His sake,*
> *that we may live a disciplined, righteous and godly life,*
> *to the glory of Your holy name. Amen.*[4]

Not a spell to clear the charges, but a fragile confession before the one who sees.

Selah.

THE LORD IS
KNOWN
BY THE JUDGMENT

THE WICKED IS SNARED
IN THE WORK

HE EXECUTES

OF HIS OWN HANDS

Abuse of power

The wicked shall be turned into hell,
And all the nations that forget God.
For the needy shall not always be forgotten;
The expectation of the poor shall not perish forever.

PSALM 9, VERSES 17 AND 18

It's the mildest form of swearing we've got: "hell." It gets no social media banning, and, at worst, there may be a raised eyebrow from a great-aunt. Yet place this word in a sacred text and, I'll admit, I shudder. Perhaps because it feels judgmental, final. We hope for kindness, for eternal grace.

When the layers are peeled back from these terrifying words, they reveal a haunting logic—track with me a minute. To choose a life without reference to a higher being is every human's right. If, at the conclusion of that life, the higher being would force you to come under his rule, in his domain, *that* would be an abuse of power, a dismissal of the order of things. For you can't set up free will for life

and then trounce it when breath is gone! That's obscene. If, however, there is no afterlife, these are dismissible fables and fairy tales.

But this ancient writer believed that there was more, and I'm drawing out his song!

The future of each life, he writes, comes from the course each person sets. Where God is dismissed, that choice will be honored: He will remain at a distance in death. The choice will be met with integrity. But for those who leaned in for help, who moved close through their days, they'll be welcomed into His home. The proximity carries through.

There's a balance to it; each choice made is remembered. For if death is just a flicker in the life of our eternal soul, surely the decisions made on one side of it would be honored on the other? Otherwise, there is great treachery in the heart of Omnipotence.

Skyscrapers and canyons

Arise, O LORD,
Do not let man prevail;
Let the nations be judged in Your sight.
Put them in fear, O LORD,
That the nations may know themselves to be but men.
Selah

PSALM 9, VERSES 19 AND 20

We'd finished sixteen weeks of essays and debate. Spiritual Formation was my degree and finger formation appeared to be the means of getting it! It seemed like calluses were forming on the tips of each digit as I tapped the tasks onto the screen. But "send" had been pressed on the last assignment, and we were heading west. High-rises, sparkling culture, and the clamor of the city softened in the rearview mirror. The reflection was traded for vast deserted spaces, redwoods and rapids, cliffs and canyons. Five weeks of nature on full volume—deafening, silent, overwhelming the senses.

The morning came when we set the GPS for home. It was daunting as we remembered the hugeness of the city, the height and weight of it all. After thousands of miles, in the evening haze, we saw the familiar Chicago skyline— the Hancock, Trump, and Willis Towers. But they were tiny! In the light of what we'd seen, the skyscrapers were pencil lines at the bottom of a broad page. (Do you see them in the image? I've drawn them in light and small.)

As I read through the verses, my memory placed me in the passenger seat of our little blue van, "that the nations may know themselves to be but men," small marks on a wide sheet. That perspective-bringing, oxygen-infusing trip allowed me to enjoy the fact that I am not that important!

The warrior-poet asks for humility in those warring against him. Not that they'd cower in David's presence, but for something far more significant. That they would see the smallness of their power and bow down before the Most High.

ARISE O LORD ARISE

do not let man prevail do not let man prevail do not let man prevail do not let man prevail do not let man prevail do not let man prevail do not let man prevail do not let man prevail do not let man prevail do not let man prevail do not let man prevail do not let man prevail do not let man prevail do not let man prevail do

Let the nations be judged in Your sight put them in fear O Lord Let the nations be judged

to be   but   men

THAT THE NATIONS MAY KNOW THEMSELVES THAT THE NATIONS MAY KNOW THEMSELVES THAT THE NATIONS MAY KNOW THEMSELVES THAT

Why Are You Far Away? — A Lament of David

What happened? What provoked such accusation? What took place to make the psalmist feel God had walked out of town? We sense his unease, his fear at being forgotten. He even crafts the chaos he feels into the structure of the song, breaking the acrostic he began in Psalm 9 to show his disorientation.

It is perhaps helpful we don't know the history of this song, of what happened to prompt its composition. For if we knew, we might offer solutions. We'd perhaps find ways to stop David from saying he's been abandoned, help him soften the words to take off the edge. He mustn't say that God hides when life gets hard; that's rude and unbecoming for a disciple. We'd likely bring piety to the table, remind him God is always with us and to remember the medicine of theology and praise that he took in Psalm 8.

But we have no history to analyze, we've only hollowed emotion, a soul crying into the void. His words sink into the soft places in us, for we have been in this place, dug out, disappointed, undefended, alone.

It can be difficult to voice our questions in this boisterous world.

The Wednesday night Bible study began with friendship and coffee; noisy camaraderie filled up the space. With the opening of Bibles, discussion stiffened. Each person worried they might let something slip that would cast doubt on the contentment of their life with God. Someone sneezed, then caught the smile of his football buddy opposite. The leader's question was still unanswered as the clock chimed the half hour: "Describe your relationship with God. Does He seem near or far away?" Here was an invitation to authenticity. Would the group go beyond what was expected? Tom decided to take the risk and speak out of his unease. For years he'd known that God was close; each morning he sensed His with-ness. But the last few months, he felt adrift. He had made no changes to the way he followed, but everything was different. It was like God had left.

Tom's vulnerable words rested between them. How would they be received? From the patterned couch came the first response: "You must have done something, mate. What did you do?" Ah, that's what would happen, that's the way this would go; his life would be questioned, his actions probed. All eyes fixed on Tom, as the group retreated behind a collective screen. This is how they learned to bury their fears, to put covers over their doubts.

There is no hint that David did anything to cause a rift between him and the Almighty. Silence from heaven doesn't signify sin. What we have in Psalm 10 is a reflection on injustice and a weak soul waiting for aid.

Without David's record of this experience, we'd have little help with our unanswered prayers, or with those one-sided conversations that litter dark seasons or the gaps in our five-year plans. This is no time to fix, to criticize or condemn. It is a time for the wrestle of Psalm 10.

David came empty to face unthinkable crimes. There is enough menace in these verses to script a psychological horror film. And there's beauty that baffles in its carefree contrast. Extremes of description are woven together in the same three hundred words.

But how can panic meet peace? How can the faith David holds and the creed he follows be intact as he watches the ruthless get away with whatever they like?

Don't come with trite assurances that "it's a broken world." What solace does that bring when teddy bear curtains gust through the bombed out windows of toddlers' bedrooms? What comfort is that to the Albanian teen, offered a modeling career near her dad's market stall only to wake in a red light district without passport or language or hope? Families crumble while the wicked clothe themselves with Lamborghinis and gold. Easy answers grate; shallow platitudes shred our souls. In the dread of their night, when they called to God, He didn't bring any help. These are the moments when faith is ousted, when people abandon the church.

But how can the psalmist in these short verses move from isolation and terror to songs of jubilant praise? Has he lost his mind?

No, he's still got all his faculties! David's approach to the dilemma he's in is profound. It holds value for us; it has weight.

In this psalm, David does two things: he looks at his situation, and he looks at his God. There is no flinching in either direction. He neither belittles the despair nor excuses the Almighty. Yes, the situation is critical; and yes, God is powerful—these two truths stand. Neither are treated as less than they are.

His assessment of the wicked is blazingly astute. Their injustice flows from arrogance—in their thoughts (verse 4), words (verse 6), and deeds (verse 8). In pride, they stand tall over nations. Their contempt for Yahweh in verses 3 and 11 brackets this detailed description of their stance.

The anguish of David's present does not intimidate his faith. Nor does it lessen his pleas for the Almighty to move from heaven through his door, to step in and make it right. He shows astonishing freedom in speaking with God. That his Friend has not intervened is excruciating; but belief that God knows what He's doing allows the psalmist to entreat and accept, plead and endure. His earnest request does not threaten the connection.

And when change doesn't happen and the mess stays the same, David considers what is true—God is aware of each shame that spreads its bruise into history, and at the end of days, each wound will be remembered. There will be a reckoning.

So he brings his strong praise to the King of all kings, whose attention and intent span the epochs of time, and in whose eternal presence, all will be made right.

To be frank

Why do You stand afar off, O LORD?
Why do You hide in times of trouble?

PSALM 10, VERSE 1

There's nothing quite like a friend by our side, who knows our story, who's intrigued by our days; it is sunshine through rain! But when trouble comes and that friend's out of reach, we can feel indistinct, blurred.

Trouble had come. The writer of this ancient songbook has much to say on the matter. He takes most of the psalm to map the terror, but in this verse, he begins with what's crushing him.

David needs his Friend to stand between him and the strife, to hold back the advance and give him air. All could be made new with a mere thought from the heavens, but God is nowhere to be found.[1] We hear his ache yelled into the darkness.

The sentiment reaches our night. These words might never come from our mouths, but on empty days they can flash into our thoughts: *God, You seem a million miles away. Are You hiding? I need you to bring help. To be help. Where are You?*

I think He's okay with our being blunt. Friends are.

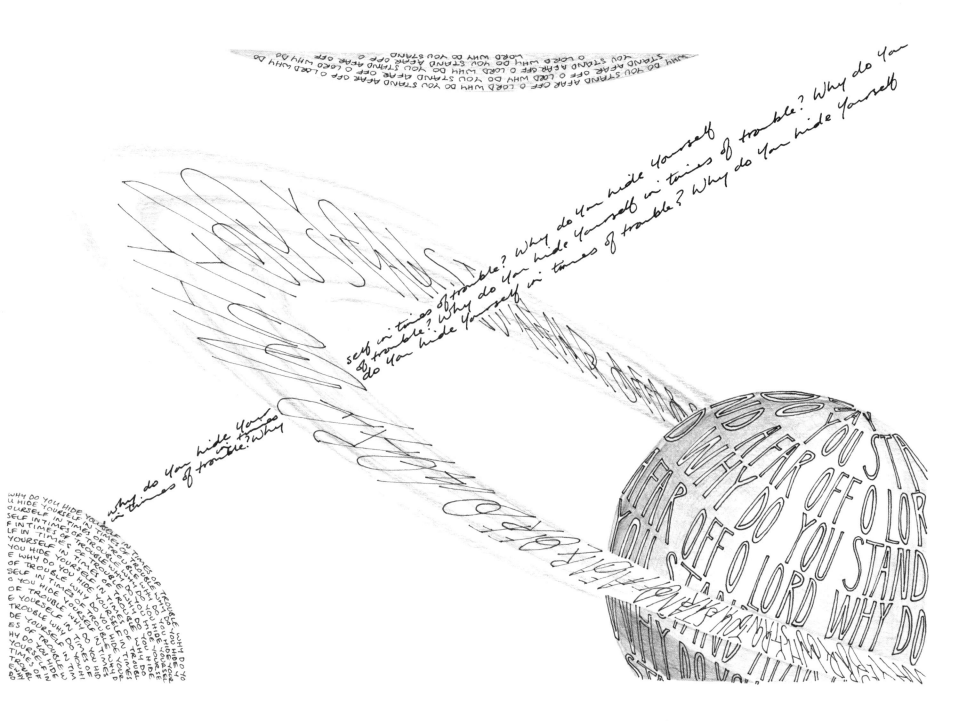

An intervention

The wicked in his pride persecutes the poor;
Let them be caught in the plots which they have devised.

PSALM 10, VERSE 2

David stands alone, scanning the horizon, singing a dirge across the expanse. The lower notes rumble through hate and oppression, lending gloom to the minor key.

He creates the tune and teaches others the lines. The volume swells to make sure that his Friend in the distance is in no doubt that intervention is way overdue. And he waits.

Yesterday, I met someone working with slaves. (I hate that that sentence is possible. It should have been over in the 1800s; it should have never begun. But the ruthless still purchase the poor.) The cadence of our conversation differed from ordinary chat. Spaces grew longer between the stories, as despair rose and as hope waned . . . for the wide-eyed teenager living on dog food. Selah. For the curly haired Syrian girl in a locked cupboard. Selah. How could the proud so degrade the weak? Images of shame punched breath from our lungs.

David's rage at injustice is ours.

What he needs lies beyond his power to act. But One with all authority could reverse their schemes and throw the oppressors into their cupboards. He asks God to trap the arrogant in the shame that they've devised. David asks God to make them fall.

A fair amount of swagger

For the wicked boasts of his heart's desire;
He blesses the greedy and renounces the LORD.
The wicked in his proud countenance does not seek God;
God is in none of his thoughts.

PSALM 10, VERSES 3 AND 4

Light dims as the wicked gloat about their greed and circle around their cravings. They name the greedy, "sacred"; they bless their lusts.

Dignity, compassion, and kindness are out, and a new religion is installed. It crowns the god of "self." There's a fair amount of swagger.

This doesn't feel safe.

I heard about four friends who were watching a play. They found it wooden and dull and were getting upset that they'd paid a great deal for such a poor show. Deciding to lodge their dislike of the act, they considered their options: they could walk out, shout out, or leave a poor review. They opted to shower the performance with scorn. In the middle of Act 1, with polite, "excuse me's," the four moved along their row to the aisle. They began to chat with each other as they mounted the stage. Pulling on coats, laughing and joking, they crossed the platform as if the actors weren't there! They walked right through the play. The contempt was loud; you couldn't miss the sneer.

The people in this song opt to ridicule. They mock the Creator, His design, His intent. They walk through the middle of His creation, treating Him as wholly irrelevant. God is in none of their thoughts.

Where's my sticker?

His ways are always prospering;
Your judgments are far above, out of his sight;
As for all his enemies, he sneers at them.
He has said in his heart,
"I shall not be moved;
I shall never be in adversity."
His mouth is full of cursing and deceit and oppression;
Under his tongue is trouble and iniquity.

PSALM 10, VERSES 5 TO 7

There's a creed that's elemental; it's at the base of our society: the good will prosper, the wicked, fail. It seems harmless enough. It encourages morality, values virtue, and keeps the kids in line!

So we run after the dream of a life that is blessed. We modify our behavior and suppress our dissent. And when success comes, we may think that God smiles on our goodness. For our comfort is surely His sign of approval on our choices, on our family and our friends.

This mantra is poison wrapped up with a bow!

When we look around from this self-oriented stance, we see random favor bestowed on all. The partying neighbor has the business win, while the mother who strives is left destitute. The drug dealer on the corner drives the fast car, while the young doctor is paralyzed by MS. The code is not being followed; the system isn't fair. And doubts rise about a God who doesn't seem to know about *our* good and *their* bad, *our* virtue and *their* deceit, who isn't following the rules we agreed on at the beginning of this game.

But those weren't the rules.

Is there some other plan at play in the universe, a different system and order of things? Surely, being good should get the stickers! Even the kids know that.

YOUR JUDGEMENTS ARE FAR ABOVE OUT OF HIS SIGHT

HIS WAYS   ARE ALWAYS   PROSPERING

ALWAYS PROSPERING   HIS   WAYS ARE   ALWAYS   PROSPERING

                        ALWAYS PROSPERING   ALWAYS   WAYS ARE

PROSPERING   HIS WAYS   ARE ALWAYS PROSPERING   WAYS ARE ALWAYS   HIS   WAYS ARE

                                          PROSPERING   PROSPERING   ALWAYS   HIS WAYS ARE ALWAYS
HIS WAYS ARE ALWAYS PROSPERING   HIS WAYS ARE ALWAYS
        HIS   WAYS   ARE ALWAYS   PROSPERING   HIS WAYS   ARE ALWAYS
PROSPERING   PROSPERING   ALWAYS   PROSPERING HIS WAYS
ARE ALWAYS PROSPERING   HIS WAYS ARE   ALWAYS PROSPERING
        ALWAYS PROSPERING HIS WAYS   ALWAYS PROSPERING HIS WAYS ARE
HIS WAYS ARE ALWAYS PROSPERING HIS WAYS ARE   HIS WAYS ARE ALWAYS   ALWAYS
        HIS WAYS ARE ALWAYS   PROSPERING

Tea and scones

He sits in the lurking places of the villages;
In the secret places he murders the innocent;
His eyes are secretly fixed on the helpless.
He lies in wait secretly, as a lion in his den;
He lies in wait to catch the poor;
He catches the poor when he draws him into his net.
So he crouches, he lies low,
That the helpless may fall by his strength.
He has said in his heart,
"God has forgotten;
He hides His face;
He will never see."

PSALM 10, VERSES 8 TO 11

The image darkens and the story gets sinister. This is no cozy mystery solved over tea and scones with some moral finger wagging. The atmosphere prickles with evil as deep shadows fall on the poor, as the innocent are marked for destruction. The darkness he describes has all the hallmarks of genocide.

The bass line vibrates that there is no one to answer.

These words are sacred text? Yes. And the massacre is set to music. There's stalking, lurking, hunting, and capture. It puts Hitchcock on the bench. Contempt has escalated from belittling the weak to destroying their dignity, crushing the breath from their lives.

In it all, the tyrant acknowledges a higher power but declares Him impotent, forgetful, and scared. The words are gruesome, fueled by hate, ten verses of desolation.

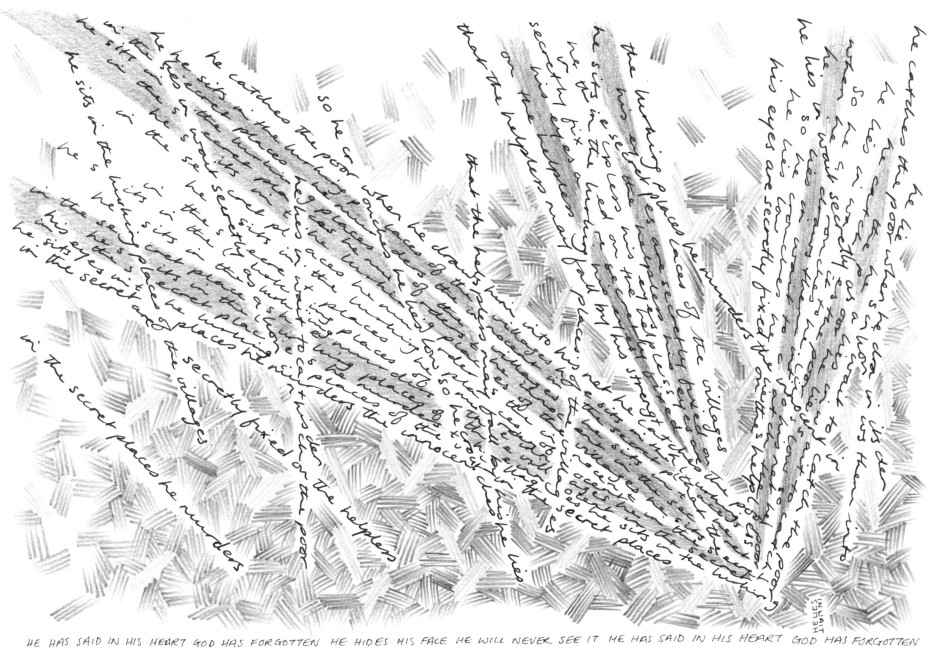

HE HAS SAID IN HIS HEART GOD HAS FORGOTTEN HE HIDES HIS FACE HE WILL NEVER SEE IT HE HAS SAID IN HIS HEART GOD HAS FORGOTTEN

Identity theft

Arise, O LORD!
O God, lift up Your hand!
Do not forget the humble.
Why do the wicked renounce God?
He has said in his heart,
"You will not require an account."

PSALM 10, VERSES 12 AND 13

In the mind of the wicked, David writes, God is pointless. He's to be rejected as a hostile schoolmaster, restricting our pleasure, suppressing the spirit.

David has an altogether different view. He'd met the Lord in the darkness and discovered God was *for* him; the friendship he found was pure gold. The Almighty was no vengeful dictator; He'd stepped into the psalmist's shame and washed his wounds.

So why should the wicked discard His compassion? Why scorn someone who can bring peace? I suspect it's a case of mistaken identity, of believing God to be a vengeful critic. They've mistaken His values as paths to weakness, for selflessness could make days inconvenient and honesty could cut through cash profits.

The path that they take is to reject His ethics. They choose arrogance over virtue, power over beauty; holding up hollow tin trophies and missing the gold—for David's life is enriched a hundredfold in character and a thousandfold in settled peace. Thus, with confidence he turns to the God who sees him and asks Him to act in a situation that's out of control.

Rocks in the ocean

But You have seen, for You observe trouble and grief,
To repay it by Your hand.
The helpless commits himself to You;
You are the helper of the fatherless.
Break the arm of the wicked and the evil man;
Seek out his wickedness until You find none.

PSALM 10, VERSES 14 AND 15

These words speak of commitment and movement toward One who is strong. I had been thinking through the lines while sitting by the sea in Edinburgh, Scotland. The evening golden hour had begun. Families around fell silent, their eyes fixed on the glowing waters as the sun put on her dazzling display. A little boy ran to the shoreline, lobbing a rock into the gilded sea. All our eyes crinkled at his joy—that rock was all in, committed! No part of it was dry; each plane connected to the current, it was now part of something vast.

And that is what I drew—"the helpless *commits* himself to You," wholly entrusted to the "helper of the fatherless." All in.

A father in Bible culture defends those who have no status; children and daughters gather to him for protection; without dads, they're left wide open to all kinds of abuses. The role that God takes is powerful protector, ready to break the bones of cruel opportunists. Does that sound strong? *Yes*! And I love it! There have been times since my dad died that I wished for this side of his presence, to march into places of neglect and injustice and knock heads together.

But the Eternal Father isn't hindered by death, for He never leaves the present. He is fully aware, sees *all* of the grief. And a day will arrive when He'll stand against the thugs, be they ever so well dressed, to restore dignities and avenge the disgrace.

Faith whispers

The LORD is King forever and ever;
The nations have perished out of His land.
LORD, You have heard the desire of the humble;
You will prepare their heart;
You will cause Your ear to hear,
To do justice to the fatherless and the oppressed,
That the man of the earth may oppress no more.

PSALM 10, VERSES 16 TO 18

How does the poet go from verse one to this? From absence to presence? He's shouting out declarations of kindness, of peace. Did everything change? Did God answer and show up? Is it all better now?

I doubt it! I suspect he's still feeling the distance. His faith is based not on his reading of God's actions, but on His character. He said He will hear, so David declares it. He has shown He is just, so the song sings it out. The duration of His goodness is measured in eons, while those who caused all the heartache become one with the dust.

This praise is not drummed up emotional hype. He is kneeling in the alley where the crushed find shelter, but his heart is in the heavens, for this is not the final word. It's tough to speak hope into the night when we don't feel it, or can't see it. But it's not the end of the story. It's just not!

And faith, even whispered, speaks light into shadows and hope into gloom.

THE LORD IS KING FOREVER AND EVER AND EVER FOREVER AND EVER FOREVER FO

TO DO JUSTICE TO THE FATHERLESS AND THE OPPRESSED TO DO JUSTICE TO THE FATHERLESS JUSTICE AND THE OPPRESSED TO DO JUSTICE TO THE FATHER TO DO JUSTICE AND THE OPPRESSED TO DO JUSTICE TO THE FATHERLESS AND THE AND THE AND THE OPPRESSED

LORD YOU HAVE HEARD THE DESIRE OF THE HUMBLE LORD YOU HAVE HEARD YOU HAVE HEARD YOU WILL PREPARE THEIR HEARTS YOU

that the man of the earth may oppress no more   no more.

PSALM 11

Trust in God, the Hater of Violence— A Lament of David

We moved to beautiful Cambridgeshire, England, after Adrian finished his studies. The winters there didn't lend themselves to outdoor skating—for that you'd need the icy north of Wisconsin, where towns are built on water. So, when the small lake near us had ducks standing on the surface, watching their food swim up to taunt their webbed feet, teenagers flocked to the spot, flinging their parents' old skates over their shoulders. We watched their tentative shuffling with arms firmly linked, squealing as they edged from the frozen reeds. The ice held, and they slowly ventured farther, when a little girl skimmed through their hesitations to glide clear across the middle! Not to be outdone by the tiny child, they embarked on her confident route. But they were bigger, had seen more summers, the ice complained loudly at their heady advance. They scrabbled hastily back to the edge as the blond four-year-old floated back. The foundation they were hoping would hold them refused to carry their play.

Foundations. They're our prerequisite for movement, for joy, for any amount of living. We disregard the ground, take it entirely for granted, for what is beneath our feet will surely be solid—it has always been so.

The words in the center of this lament are not just a phrase, they're a destabilization ("If the foundations are destroyed, what can the righteous do?" [verse 3]). Nothing can be done if the ground is not safe. From this place of paralysis, David's companions school him. Retreat, run for the mountains, the earth is giving way. There is nothing that the righteous can do.

They try everything to convince him to flee. They cite terrifying gangsters hidden in the undergrowth, invisible troops gaining ground. It is his soldiers' *sight* that brings in the panic; visions of plots and hidden assassins expand in their brains to become all they can see! The only sensible choice is to run to find refuge. The puzzle is why their leader is not alarmed.

David names another unseeable force. God needs no cover to screen Him from view and no foundation to hold Him steady. He is Lord over nature; He is king over creatures; He reigns over the breadth of the heavens. From beginning to end (verses 1 and 7), all are under His watch, be they concealed or in plain sight.

There is something in this poetic journal that I have found exceptional, time after time. When David's throat is clamped by fear, the Almighty fills his mind. And when his chest swells to fit in all the joy, the Lord is right before him. Whether on a dusty track or a palace step, in each direction he turns, God is the oxygen of his life, the One who fills every possible path. It's striking.

We moved to rural Derbyshire, where Mr. Darcy's Pemberley Hall[1] (Chatsworth House) is cradled by soft fields, small hamlets, and gentle people. We were fresh out of Bible college. Our task was to help groups of Christ followers in the eighteenth-century Methodist chapels speckling the countryside; we were to carry the inspiring teaching of Jesus of Nazareth. It was daunting to have this as our full-time endeavor. It challenged our British reserve.

We gathered at Barton-in-the-Beans one weekend, meeting community leaders, congregations, and kind well-wishers. Balancing cups, saucers, and scones, a Swiss gentleman moved toward us nodding a silent hello. He looked up into Adrian's face, opening with, "Being an evangelist is easy. I've been one for years." This was a line that surprised us. "Just let people into your life," he continued. "When life's hard, let them see where you run for your refuge, when it's great, let them see where you go to for joy. Let people see that Jesus is amazing!" We looked into his mellow, peaceful face. Each direction he looked he found rest with his eternal Friend. His shoulders shrugged a smile, and he melted into the crowd.

David's God was his constant, in the dark days and in the light. So, we can understand his consternation: Why run for help to desert rocks when the Almighty is right here?

John Chrysostom's fourth-century commentary takes up his song: "I have the Lord of the universe as my ally. The One who without difficulty created everything everywhere is my leader and support, and you would send me to the wilderness and provide for my safety in the desert? After all, surely the help from the desert does not surpass the One capable of anything with complete ease?"[2]

David is looking at two powers: the wicked, smug in the center, firing their threats at the righteous; and the God who sees, El Roi, right above their heads. What we see in the psalm is justice meted out in a manner that can be described as ingenious. God surrounds those who love violence, and destroys them by their own hand. It's an ambush where they dole out the punishment! And in their arrogance they don't see it coming.

This incredible song is a wholehearted trust in the integrity of God. It's the psalm that Athanasius wrote: "If anyone wishes to disturb you, hold on strongly to your confidence in the Lord and say Psalm 11."

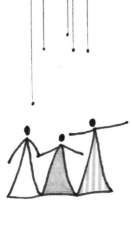

Seeing in the dark

In the LORD I put my trust;
How can you say to my soul,
"Flee as a bird to your mountain"?
For look! The wicked bend their bow,
They make ready their arrow on the string,
That they may shoot secretly at the upright in heart.

PSALM 11, VERSES 1 AND 2

The situation's threatening with danger all around. Crack troops pursue them, set to end David's life. There seemed no way out of the darkness. With this in play, his warrior-companions brought their considered, sage advice..

RUN!

David, we're in crisis! Get jets under your wings! There are enemies in the bushes firing arrows from the darkness. We have to flee. We need to find cover.

Fear feeds their counsel, and panic sets their course, as they chase after rumors of refuge. And you wonder, just wonder, would there be shelter in those mountains or rest for their souls? Or would panic push them to the next peak, and the next, at whispers of a firmer fortress?

David stands still. He calls them out. To find peace in mountains is chasing after the wind. Rest is not found in the contours of the country. He has found the location of safety. It's in Someone who can see in the dark.

Swords on the ground

If the foundations are destroyed,
What can the righteous do?

PSALM 11, VERSE 3

It's late afternoon as the radio's gloomy news broadcast triggers the lyrics of a rap song in my brain. The artist asks where values, fairness, and love have gone; that their place in society is taken away by destructive forces that lead us far from goodness and far from peace.[3]

Today's verse chimes right in. Truth. Honesty. Valor. Family. The bedrocks of society have been shattered. Saul has taken virtue and ground it in the dirt; he's found power in violence and strength in deceit.

David's advisers and friends hear news from their homeland that's a wrecking ball to their hearts. They turn to him, lamenting, *There is no place for us here. It is time to retreat. There is nothing the righteous can do.*

They map out a future of withdrawal from the mess: sever from society and keep safe till the end. In the mountains, they can set standards of honor and value truth, but the answer to what's happening is to run far away.

And we get it. When our community frays, when its fabric unravels, hope lies silent in the empty dark. When those we trusted spit out hate, those we respected trample us in gutters, despair seems a viable option. What's the point of carrying on?

That is where we find David's soldiers. Swords on the ground, hearts in the dirt.

IF THE
FOUNDATIONS
ARE DESTROYED

what can the righteous do?

Where you're held

The LORD is in His holy temple,
The LORD's throne is in heaven;
His eyes behold,
His eyelids test the sons of men.

PSALM 11, VERSE 4

David's companions are begging to flee for the mountains, escape the peril, find somewhere safe. But the warrior-shepherd has met danger before. Lions have tracked him on lonely hillsides, bears have leapt out to devour his life. So rather than racing for distant rocks, he stands still.

He offers his friends some thoughts on stability.

Peace is about far more than location; we find rest in the place where we're held. We need someone unmoved by treachery or rattled by legions of fighters. We need someone unshakable. David looks up. The rule of the Almighty is fixed in the heavens; it will not fade or fail. From His throne, justice and strength cascade. He is there. He stands firm, forever.

The shepherd's song rises. Yes, despair is available, but why waste the energy when his Eternal companion sees all from His immortal throne?

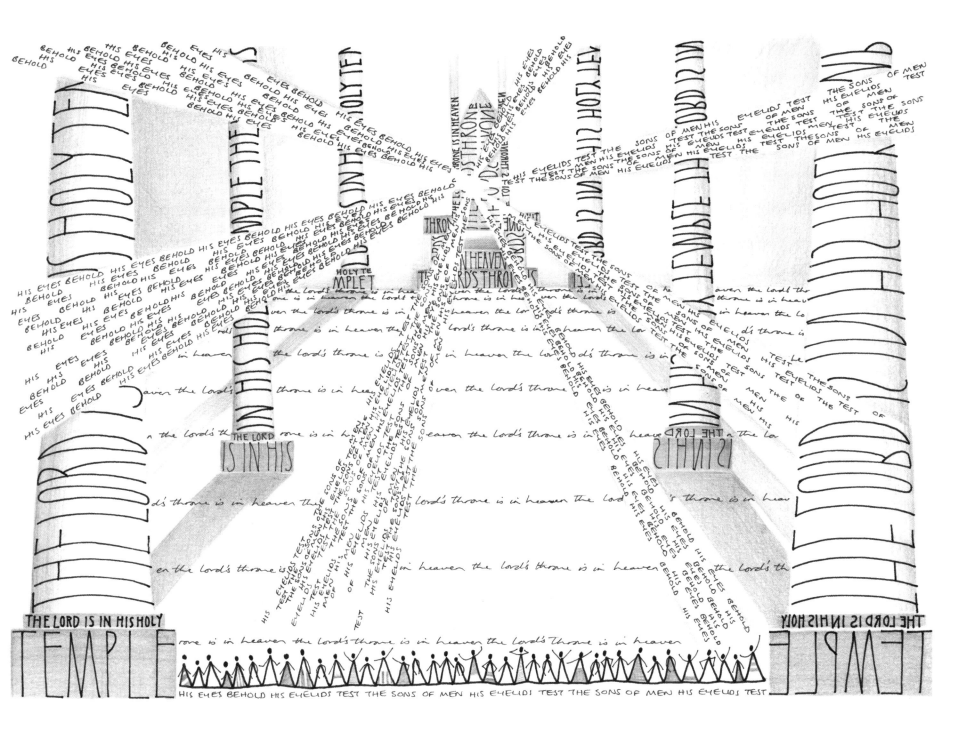

Church mischief

The LORD tests the righteous,
But the wicked and the one who loves violence
His soul hates.
Upon the wicked He will rain coals;
Fire and brimstone and a burning wind
Shall be the portion of their cup.

PSALM 11, VERSES 5 AND 6

When we lived in Chicago, we visited a huge church with columns. The edifice spread over manicured lawns. Immaculate children clasped Bibles in covers as they filed with patient parents along mahogany pews. The ceremony was impeccable; the choreography, perfection! So why was I fighting the urge to trip up the usher with his platter of cash? I wanted to see what was beneath the theater. Would he swear at me, smile, or remain as austere as his stern three-piece suit? (Adrian saw the mischief in me and with dancing eyes, mouthed, "Noooooo!")[4]

The thing about masks is we can't *see* the person; even generous gestures can hide malicious intent. "Villainy wears many masks, none so dangerous as the mask of virtue."[5] To discover who is foe and who is friend, we need a test to show what's on the inside.

And that's where we are in David's song—the One crowned in the heavens sees through skin as through glass. He tests people so that *they* can see who they are. And those filled with burning and violence and hate? He says they'll be met with the same. Their environment will match their souls; chaos will be their lot.

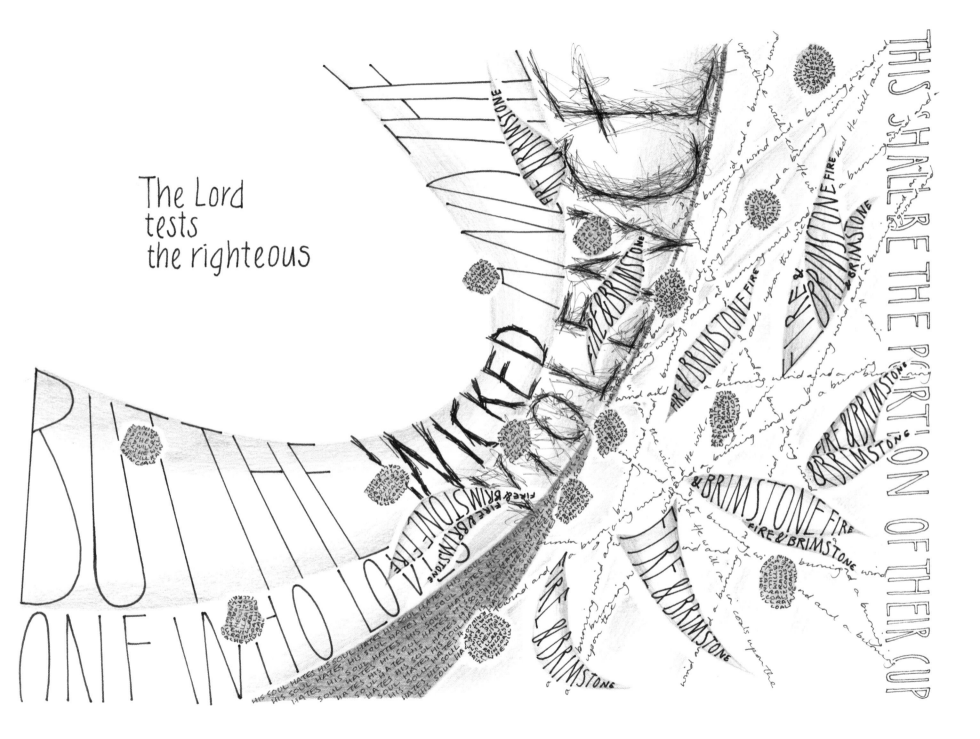

The Lord
tests
the righteous

Climate change

For the LORD is righteous,
He loves righteousness;
His countenance beholds the upright.

PSALM 11, VERSE 7

When we want to make ourselves clearer, we may repeat a line. But to speak the words a third time is doing something more—we're underlining, highlighting, and mic-dropping our point! We are making a statement.

We have here a three-thousand-year-old description of the essence of the Creator: He is righteous. We then move to the area of emotions: He loves righteousness. We finally come to what He does: He beholds the righteous. The storyline is the same in all three.

Righteous. David can't find a better word.

I went to the thesaurus to get a sense of its meaning, and the spread was sublime! Honorable, ethical, noble, good, fair, just, kind, faithful. The words, in beauty, stretched out.

With these two syllables, the climate shifts from fear and flight to stillness.

And he is well.

RGHTEOUS

He LOVES righteousness

HIS COUNTENANCE BEHOLDS THE UPRIGHT HIS COUNTENANCE

The Vanishing of Goodness—
A Lament of David

Minister and civil right advocate Dr. John M. Perkins wrote that "the psalms of lament were meant to be tools in the community worship experience to bring the worshipers into the presence of our God. The lament is His gift to us, His church. They urge us to come and be healed together."[1]

David's community is dazed by deceit, battered down by lies. He stands on behalf of the nation, calling the Almighty to act. His lament is about words—these patterns of breath from the core of creatures that intensely impact our living. Words that bring carnage, extinguish hope, and fill homes with fear; and words that speak truth, bind up pain, and allow us to dream.

David starts with hyperbole, overstating the disaster to get heaven's attention. *Evil is everywhere. Good people are vanishing. The situation couldn't be any more dire.*

The next four verses seem to be oversharing! It sounds as if David hasn't picked up on the rules: there are acceptable and unacceptable things we can say. This level of detail (paired with a request to mutilate his foes' faces!) sits solidly in the realm of "too much." It sounds crude; it feels weak. Good manners tell us that when disaster strikes, we should cover our stories with trust. And when we're overwhelmed and in dismay, we should dress things up with hope. We pull ill-fitting suits of pretense and acceptance over our troubled souls—it makes for more comfortable listening.

We sit in a culture where dishonesty reigns, where lies are made glorious.

Advertising shows us what we are to become, and how to cover our days with filtered lenses so we can match the media's flawless disguise. Politicians can spin things, so that every failure looks like a win. Society can trick us into believing we are casualties of our contexts, victims of the past, and not responsible for any mistakes.

And in this climate of deceit, it is very easy to lie to ourselves.

We begin to believe we don't matter and that our value is set by what others decide. We feel we protrude, so we hide who we are in order to belong. In an attempt to look normal, we bury our hurts so that we're not the one with the issues—it's tiring to keep everything spinning. And inside, we fade. We can't remember who we are. The lies have withdrawn us from friends, from God. We even feel disconnected from ourselves. "God has given you one face, and you make yourself another," wrote Shakespeare.[2] It is torment to pretend all is happy and well, that grief is trivial and anguish is small.

I came across a folder of talks last week that transported me back twenty years. Adrian and I excitedly prepared for a weeklong missions conference in the north of Scotland; we'd been asked to run the program for the teens and children. Something else was exciting us in those weeks that had us beaming from ear to ear. It still was too early to tell our family, but a baby was on the way!

Halfway through the conference, between the morning and afternoon sessions, our little one was no more. We held each other, and with broken voices brought our grief to God. We'd had joy and so much hope, and now there was nothing to share. We weren't sure what to do, for each time we left our room, children grabbed our hands, wanting

to play; teenagers wanted to talk about the sessions; and parents wanted to tell us about their concerns for their lovely young people.

Our hearts ached. But we wanted God to be seen and for us not to be a distraction, for the teachings of Jesus to be the main thing in the young people's minds. Each time we walked out of our door, we smiled, we sang, we shone, we served. And each time we walked back inside, we wept and hugged and prayed and slept. We covered over our grief and made it small so that the big things would be the most important.

And when we returned to our work and community, there was so much to do and so very many needs that we kept things quiet; we held it still. Did we do it right? I'm not sure.

I was convinced that God was far more interested in other people's spiritual lives and our service for Him than He was in our pain, more concerned by people's praise and joy rather than in our dismay. I thought it was better to focus on others so that they would be able to trust in God more. To trust Him for what, though—to be an accompaniment for tidy lives? The irony is that Jesus showed us God is strong *by* holding the weak, *by* sitting with the broken, *by* touching those overwhelmed with grief. He didn't tidy up their sorrows behind closed doors away from crowds to make them look nice. He healed them right there in the middle of it all and then gave them back to their community.

Christ moved toward hurt, was marked by compassion. He wasn't telling people to keep their heads down and blend in, to look happy and silence their pain. He wasn't interested in those who put on a performance, trying to prove that they were strong.

God seems to want truth, not make-believe. He invites our cries, sanctions our need to protest. Lament is not some feral animal growl to be silenced; it is pain faced and mourned with our heavenly Friend and woven into the fabric of our living. David scripts his trouble into a ballad that echoes haunting memories in our souls. Yes, lament is still pain, but now it is written into the fabric of our community, given space to be heard, to be sung. Lament is a gift to us.

And God's response to the messy anguish? Is He frustrated; does He look away? No, He rises to meet us. "'For the oppression of the poor, for the sighing of the needy, now I will arise,' says the LORD. 'I will set him in the safety for which he yearns.'"[3]

Vanishing act

Help, LORD, for the godly man ceases!
For the faithful disappear from among the sons of men.

PSALM 12, VERSE 1

When you wake up to the news of looting on the high street, anguished refugee camps, or terror around the globe, do you have a sense of the direction of things? Darker? Brighter? David meets a morning of escalations in abuses and is disturbed to find there are fewer people willing to stand up for what's right.

What made them vanish? What dwindled the numbers; what made the faithful sit down, the steadfast hold back?

His beliefs are no longer the view of the masses. He's in a smaller company, feeling exposed.

And his response? Does he raise his eyebrows at the outrage, grumbling, *What's the world coming to? This makes me sick.* No, that's not the option he goes for. From a dwindling group at the edge of his nation, he calls for help from One who can make a change.

Help, Lord. Good people are vanishing and the isolation's getting intense.

Help.

For the faithful disappear among the sons of men.

Losing your "brave"

They speak idly everyone with his neighbor;
With flattering lips and a double heart they speak.

May the LORD cut off all flattering lips,
And the tongue that speaks proud things,
Who have said,
"With our tongue we will prevail;
Our lips are our own;
Who is lord over us?"

PSALM 12, VERSES 2 TO 4

This three-thousand-year-old text gives an exceptional study of human character. David stands out as a scholar of the soul.

The loss of courage is not "the faithful" abandoning their convictions. He lays out his findings on how people lose courage.

It's not the enemy in the distance that makes them fall silent, but those who are by their side. The careless conversation that shifts to flattery, flattery that mutates into deceit. Lies that gain ground, pride that takes hold, and resentment that turns into defiance. And this comes from his neighbors, not random masked bandits! So the righteous sit down.

David names the treachery that splinters their souls, that divides the brave from themselves. When we are cut down by those who are closest, we are sent to live a half-life: to conform, not shine; to be silent, not stand.

What destruction empty words can bring.

MAY THE LORD CUT OFF ALL FLATTERING LIPS AND THE TONGUE THAT SPEAKS PROUD THINGS

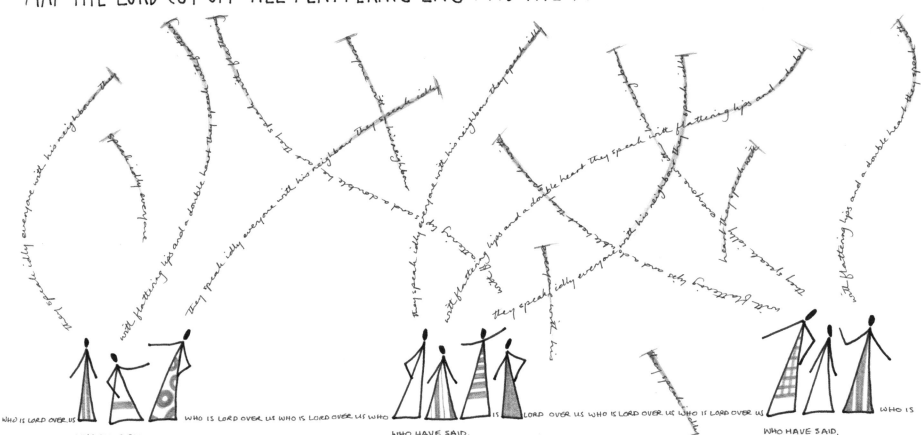

WHO IS LORD OVER US

WHO IS LORD OVER US WHO IS LORD OVER US WHO

IS LORD OVER US WHO IS LORD OVER US WHO IS LORD OVER US

WHO IS

WHO HAVE SAID,
WITH OUR TONGUE WE WILL PREVAIL
OUR LIPS ARE OUR OWN.

WHO HAVE SAID,
WITH OUR TONGUE WE WILL PREVAIL
OUR LIPS ARE OUR OWN.

WHO HAVE SAID,
WITH OUR LIPS WE WILL PREVAIL
OUR LIPS ARE OUR OWN.

Hoodies and cupcakes

"For the oppression of the poor, for the sighing of the needy,
Now I will arise," says the LORD;
"I will set him in the safety for which he yearns."

PSALM 12, VERSE 5

There is beauty in this promise that makes us catch our breath. God sees, hears, and names the impact of the trauma; it's a sensory engagement with people in distress. He calls it cruelty, poverty, and gasping need—conditions that leave the victim with no muscle to rise.

But the damage isn't done by hooded strangers with baseball bats and dire intent. It's from cheering friends holding cupcakes, frosted with betrayal and lies. The oppression comes in words spoken in the kitchen, twisting reputation, devouring character, moving with speed from flattery to hate. And trust is shattered and hearts unravel.

Here is the place where God puts His feet; this is where He shows up. His arms lift the despised from the frenzied mob and set them in the safety for which they ache.

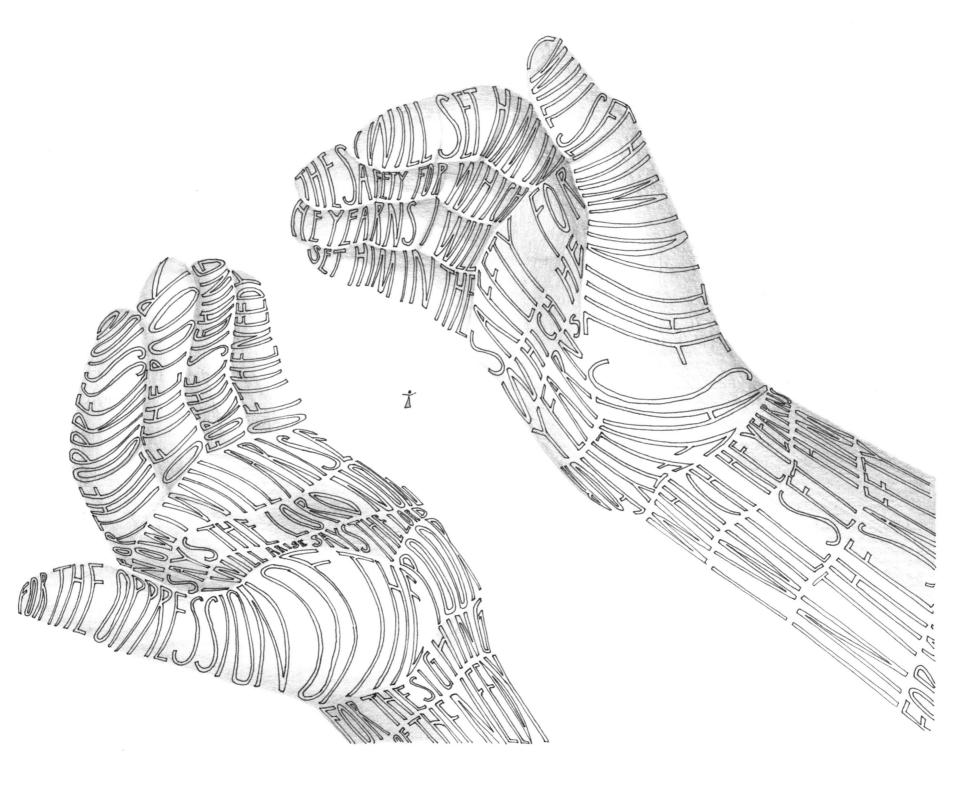

Promises, promises!

The words of the LORD are pure words,
Like silver tried in a furnace of earth,
Purified seven times.
You shall keep them, O LORD,
You shall preserve them from this generation forever.

PSALM 12, VERSES 6 AND 7

One thing that gossipers do not want is attention being paid to the details, since filtering through scorn to scrutinize sources may tell inconvenient truths. As David applies heat to the chatter around him, we sense his growing unease. Under cheering, there's deception; under praise, there is threat—and all of it stems from pride.

There can be no greater contrast between the two sets of words that are spoken in this psalm. The first, results in an ache for safety, a yearning for shielding; the helpless are caged in corners, unable to stand.

The second speaks about words that are pure, that are tested seven times. Truth holds its value—no matter how hot it gets—it destroys lies that have ruined the faithful.

The promise it ends with is not a whisper from the hopeful, but the declaration of the One who has seen all the facts. Pure words. Beauty to the maligned, rest to the scorned.

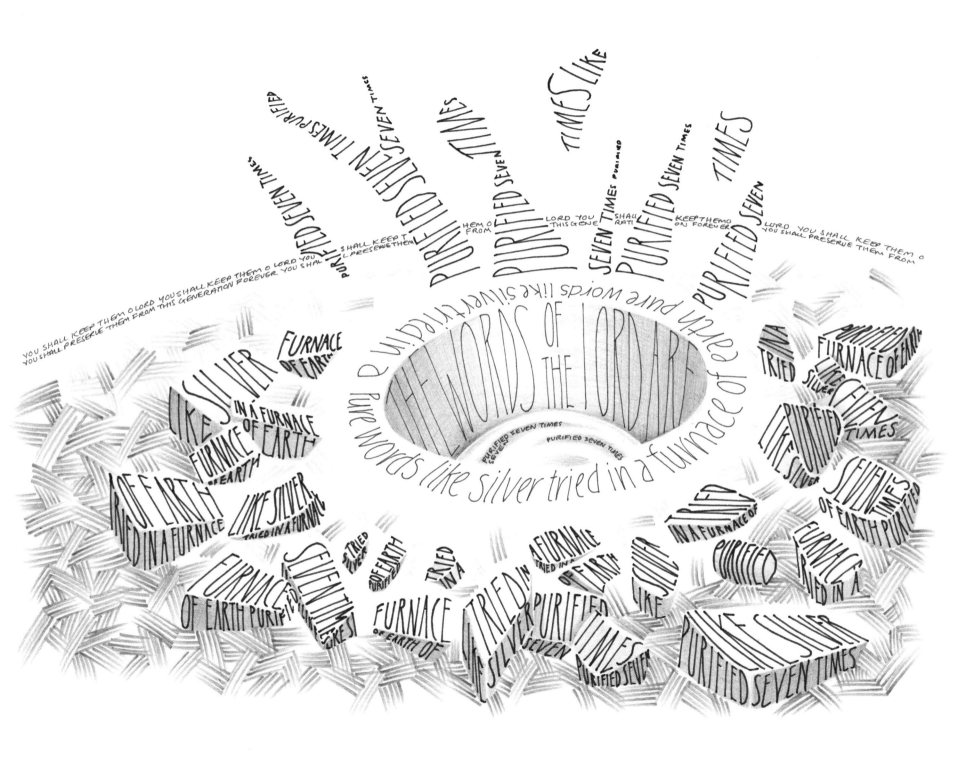

Sweating the small stuff

The wicked prowl on every side,
When vileness is exalted among the sons of men.

PSALM 12, VERSE 8

The final statement of Psalm 12's lament can stir up a lot of blustery "What's the world coming to?" rhetoric. We have heard those grumbles, and in many cases, they're fair comment—reality TV should not set our moral compass, nor should violence in our cities be the norm. But that isn't where the dreadfulness starts. It grows in harmless beginnings of empty chatter, shallow living, striving for self in a sea of need. And I wonder—If truth had been valued and honesty lifted high, would oppression be as widespread or self-centeredness as strong?

We can pass by the broken, looking down on their state, throwing judgment or advice over our shoulders. But then the words of G. K. Chesterton flicker into view. Once asked by *The Times* for an article on "What's wrong with the world?" he offered this brief and full submission: "Dear Sirs, I am."[4]

It comes home.

I've been more conscious of my words as I've drawn this week. Of the fires they can light, the damage they can cause; the small spark that exalts vileness in my defrauding little soul. We justify pulling people down, saying it was they who abused; we dismiss them for they were abhorrent. But this makes you stop. It makes you think.

The small stuff matters.

How Long? —
A Lament of David

...eep of death lest my enemy say 'I have prevailed a...

Milly was riding on the back of the quad as she and her dad took sheep feed to the higher pasture. As they passed the hill troughs, she lost hold and was thrown forward. He saw her too late. There was a short shriek as wheels flew into her bright sunflower dress. Then nothing. The farm hands down in the valley, his wife in the kitchen, a visiting vet checking a fetlock—they all heard him scream into the gray.

Five days later, the white coffin was covered in wildflowers, crowded over with their cherishing. They had waded through hymnals and lists of strong songs to choose what to sing through the torture. The family found nothing to speak for them. They were left vacant, as empty as the sky.

We need something other than praise, joy, and eternal hope when the unspeakable happens; we need more than decorative melodies to adorn our wounds. We tell lies to each other and forfeit integrity when we cover life's agonies with clichés. We need something to speak our primal aches, our "rage against the dying of the light."[1]

Psalm 13 charts that twilight rage. The poetry is tempestuous, it is raw and unnerving. It offers no platitudes to calm the bewildered. In it we hear a shattered human call out heady accusations against a God he cannot see. He charges Him with neglect, with deliberately hiding, staying in the shadows while his child's heart fails. And it seems that God's retreat from the psalmist is no momentary thing; the repeated plea "How long?" casts a hypnotic vote of no confidence.

Did the editors slip up? This song should surely be footnoted with copious explanations: *It was for then; it's not for now. It has no place in our songs of praise.* But there is no footnote, no excusing. In fact, rather than justifying God's lack of response in a tangle of knotted emotion, Psalm 13 gifts us with the template to disentangle our griefs. It is the clearest example in the Psalter of how to structure a lament.

The pattern isn't presented in steps of alliterated coaching; we walk with David through the mess. He is disoriented, for he didn't cause this. He shouts for God to show His face, to bring help into his night. The abandonment and torment are wholly undeserved, he did nothing to warrant this misery.

Alan booked a coffee with his retired pastor after a terrible week at work. He was bewildered as to why God seemed absent when this was the time He was most needed. After hearing the sermon called "Joy in Dark Times," Alan rang him up. Turning his pen absently through his fingers, he began explaining what was going on. He'd found himself whimpering on lunchtime walks, overcome by a nameless pain. He wept without warning at the gym and at the store. In the small hours, he'd wake up screaming, as terrors crept into his dreams. Despair was choking him; things were growing darker . . . he glanced up, wide open to receive his mentor's advice—what should he do? The large Bible thudded down between them as the pastor half quoted, half read many verses on sin. With a shaking head, he laid out his assessment: *You must have done something to cause this darkness. Search your heart. Find the sin.* He followed with a prayer for Alan's repentance—it felt like the air was being removed from the room. Shaken, the young man mumbled an "Amen," as the pastor nodded his dismissal and lifted the leather-bound warhead to its shelf. Troubled,

Alan left the room, pulling the door behind him.

Each night, weary from mounting victimization at work, Alan searched for some evil within. The pastor said clearly, the faults were his own. He apologized in the darkness for depravities he couldn't find.

For six months, he would drive to church, sometimes managing the first song before shame made him to slip out the back, detaching from his community, from his God, from himself—for the pastor could see what was wrong, but Alan couldn't find what he'd done.

Sin was expected; innocence was inconceivable.

If only the Bible that was used as a weapon had opened to this psalm. For it is more than an ache across the silence. As we study Psalm 13, we find that it has structure; it is arguably the best example of a how lament works in the Psalter, giving a clear pattern to follow for those who are clean out of hope.

I have written the comments that accompany the images of Psalm 13 as the template for lament. It has been of enormous personal benefit through the years in unscrambling situations with God. I commend it to you.

Choose the situation that is unsettling, and write the heading for the first step. Take time to fill in your cry before moving to Step 2. May the threads that are tangled be rewoven in the company of your Creator.

The poet stands before the Holy One, confident of innocence, inviting God's attention. Though the psalmist is shrouded in gloom, there is no question of sin or guilt. He calls, shouts, cries, speaks, and in so doing, shows the strength of the friendship. It can bear the demands, be they ever so loud. Trust is held through the confrontation, for lament is not the end of relationship, but a proof of its grit! We can stay in conversation with God through the bewildering days of life, secure in the exchange, for He's committed Himself to us. His compassion does not end.

If you're looking for a life hack to easy peace, this is not it. Psalm 13 takes us through the heart of our pain to meet God in the middle.

When young families go to a restaurant, a concert, or a church, the pressure on parents is to keep their children quiet, to make sure no young voice interrupts what's going on at the front. Silence is held up as proof of good parenting.

But there are times when silence is not golden. In 1989, when dictator Nicolae Ceaușescu was overthrown, 170,000 children were found in Romanian orphanages. On entering a hall with a hundred metal cots, you'd be forgiven for thinking them empty. The only sounds you'd hear were cars on the highway and pigeons on the roof. But every cot was occupied. The infants lay staring at walls, looking at their hands, silent. They learned after a week of tears that no one would comfort, no one would come. So they stopped asking.

Lament is God's invitation to ask the questions, tell the bloodied story; call out, muddied and wounded, to the Physician of our souls. And be heard, be tended, be healed.

The ancient path to peace

How long, O LORD? Will You forget me forever?
How long will You hide Your face from me?

PSALM 13, VERSE 1

There have been points in life where, in confusion, anger, or deep despair, I've reached for a notepad and, in a hurricane of thoughts, have worked through the process of lament. This psalm shows the five stages the clearest. They come in steps, distinct and surprising. They offer a pathway through the enigmas of life, moving us from bitterness to peace, from disillusion to hope, taking our superficiality and giving us depth.

It is a pilgrimage to wholeness.

I commend the practice to you. I have found that it works.

To prepare for the journey, there are things that you need: an undisturbed space with perhaps a little music, some water, soft clothing, paper, and a pen. Let us go gently, for there may be some blisters along the way.

The ancient writer doesn't sugarcoat his sentiments. The first two syllables carry our humanity; they quarry their way into our core. It's anguished, accusing, frustrated, raw. He cries out. I drew him in a box, alone and ignored, his prayers not piercing its ceiling.

Step 1: Cry out to God.

Choose a situation that causes discomfort, that raises questions in you. It may have occurred twenty years back, or you still may be in the thralls of it. Step one is to cry out to God. Requests will come later; this is the time for the page to fill with shouts. It is where we begin.

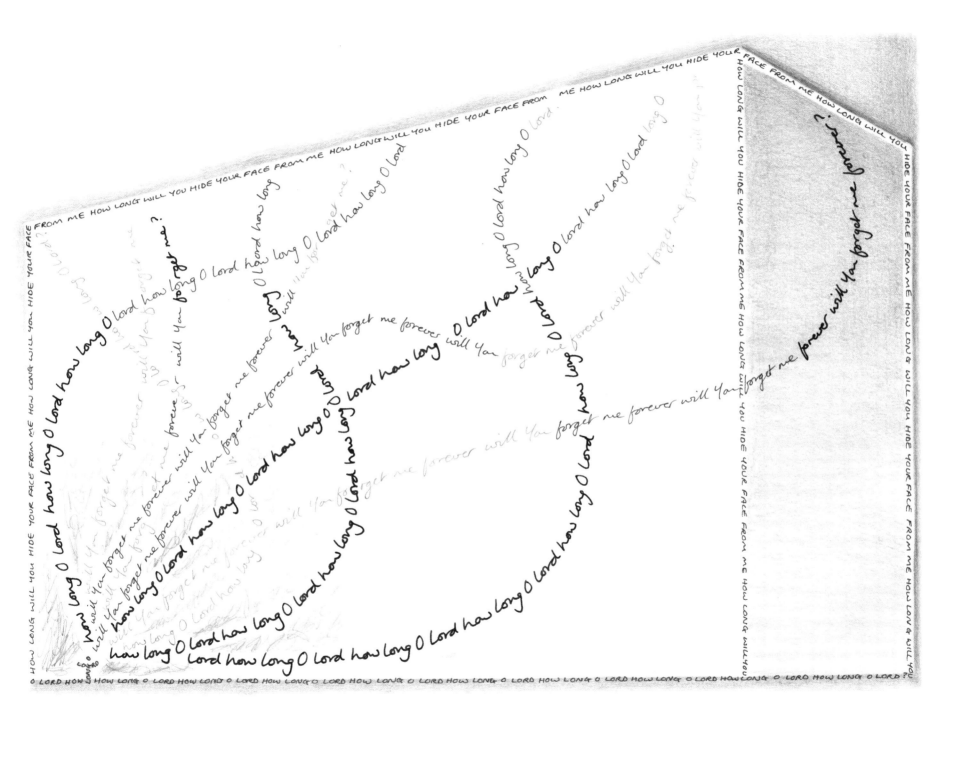

How long shall I take counsel in my soul,
Having sorrow in my heart daily?
How long will my enemy be exalted over me?

PSALM 13, VERSE 2

"He never complained." This is considered the high-water mark for undergoing suffering—that the wounded make no mention of what they're going through.

Thus, we could be tempted to move past Step 2. "Make your complaint," seems a little whiny. Should it really be a practice of the follower of God? For all the great thinkers say—work hard, take action, speak out, but lock in your sorrows. No one wants to hear them.

But here, anguish is articulated. David doesn't bottle it up, grit his teeth, stuff it down. He spells it out in words on papyrus. These lines are a protest, a deep grievance that wrestles its way across the heavens. He complains. Loudly.

There needs to be a place where torment is heard, where we can be honest and safe. This is the place; David has found it. He unlocks his sorrows to God. He lets them all pour out.

Step 2: Make your complaint.

In the situation you are pondering, write out your complaint. What it has done to you, to those around you. Where is your heart in it all?

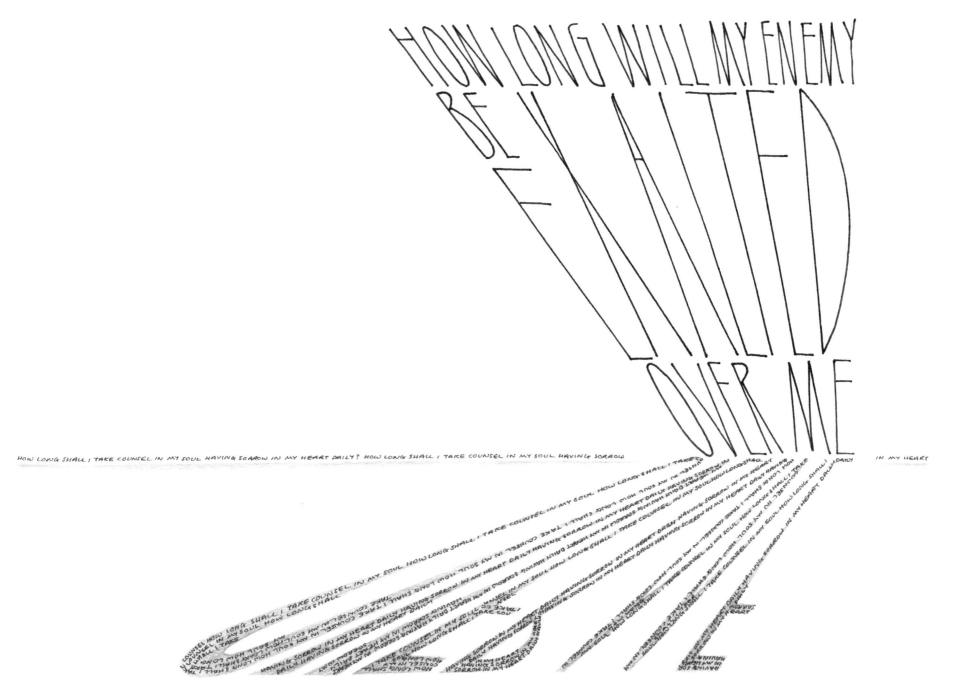

Consider and hear me, O LORD my God
Enlighten my eyes,
Lest I sleep the sleep of death;
Lest my enemy say
"I have prevailed against him";
Lest those who trouble me rejoice when I am moved.

PSALM 13, VERSES 3 AND 4

Being content with defeat was not his request. Growth and stability in his life—this was his ambition.

David's appeal takes the largest portion of his lament. He writes what he wants the Almighty to do, specifically and in detail. He needs help that lies beyond him, help that is supernatural. So he asks for it.

When we reach through the jumble to state what we want, there is an untangling.

One Tuesday morning in a full lecture hall, I asked students to take five minutes to think about what they wanted. The responses would have put apostles to shame in their aspiration and piety. The atmosphere intensified as each added more devotion to the one before. Then one student, unfazed by the direction of play said, "I want a house." There was a stunned hush at the earthiness of it. "That's it. I really really want a wee house." She spoke, unmasked from a deep longing. And I sensed the smile of God on her open heart. The space became simple and airy and light.

Step 3: Make your request.

With an open heart, what is the thing that you want God to do? What are the things you want Him to undo? Write out your true desires.

The ancient path to peace

But I have trusted in Your mercy;
My heart shall rejoice in Your salvation.

PSALM 13, VERSE 5

It has burst out—the anguish, the grief, the plea. All lie on the floor in disarray. His energy is expended. Hope has walked out the door. I love that this is in the text. It's astonishing. Most ancient writings present victories and valor, conquering kingdoms and cries for mercy. But here sits the warrior, tormented, in the mud.

And so might we be. We can find ourselves in spiraling despair.

But here the lament shifts gears. With resolve, effort, and intention, David stops the downward slide. He looks back to remember his past. He has escaped horrible jams before. He's survived failure and loss. God stepped in to be his companion, "I trusted in Your mercy." His failure hasn't been the end of the story, nor has it become his identity. God showed a mercy that David relied on—he trusted Him in the past.

In these lines, he considers his history. God has seen him through. David turns to state confidence in his eternal Friend.

Step 4: Remember the past.

Consider when God brought you through in the past. Write it down. Remember.

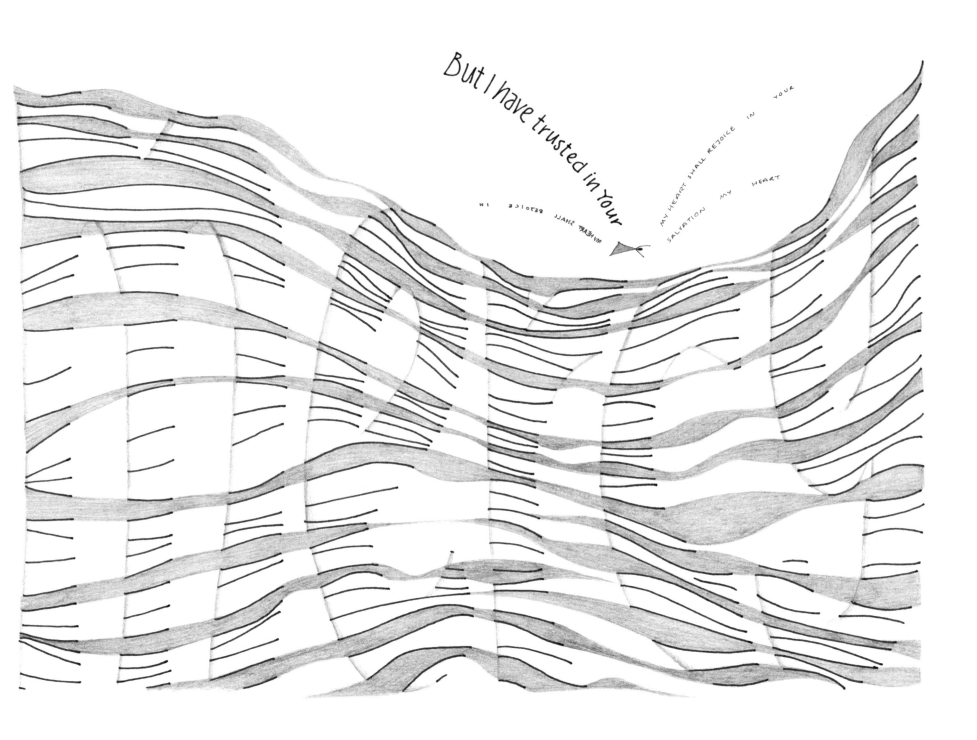

But I have trusted in Your

MY HEART SHALL REJOICE IN YOUR

MY HEART SHALL REJOICE IN

SALVATION MY HEART

The ancient path to peace

I will sing to the LORD,
Because He has dealt bountifully with me.

PSALM 13, VERSE 6

The final step in this ancient system is astonishing. David has been through tumult to process his questions. Only a few lines before, his torment ripped at our souls, "How long will You hide Your face from me?" (Psalm 13:1). Yet here he is in a place of praise?

You sing when your heart is light, when fears are in the distance and hope comes alive. So how can *David* sing?

He can sing based on what's gone before. In Step 4, David remembered God's presence in his life, rescue from trials: bears and lions mauled the sheep he tended as a teen; his best friend's father led an army to hound him around the desert; his son and companions set out to kill him, and yet, God showed him grace, mercy, and favor. He traces God's goodness in the rescues, God's companionship in disillusion. And in repeated cries for help, David has been heard. He has been seen.

And in today's mess, he is all peace.

And David sings.

The Reckless and the Refuge—
A Lament of David

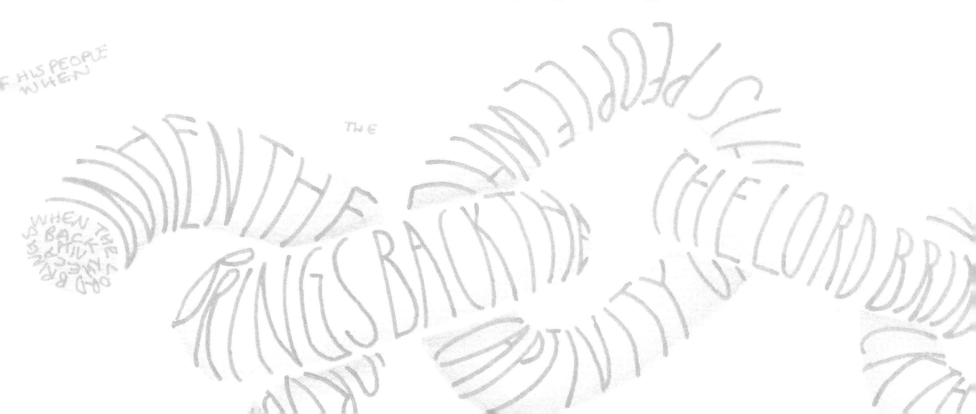

When we reach the end of a film or the last pages of a story, we expect explanations and the tying up of loose ends. The victor should be lifted, his actions admired, his values extolled as worthy, while broad men in uniform should flank the villain, removing him from the hero and the world he now enjoys.

As we reach the end of this group of psalms, it's surely reasonable to have the same expectation. This final song should resolve into peace—the wings of the dawn, green pastures, still waters, hills clothed with gladness, earth softened with showers—a basking in the goodness of the Creator. Good endings should soothe and let us know all is well.

This is not that ending!

David's song is filled with discord and yelling; there's collision and noise, not calm. His words sink far from the high point of the temple down into humanity's disgrace.

David sees oppressors as fools who run God out of town, and the lawless as arrogant wasters. The righteous are poor, broken, and needing shelter; they're hardly an advert for following God. David's phrases are thick with adrenaline and blood pressure spikes. *David, why can't we hear the choirs sing harmonies?*

Because it's not the end of the story.

The answers to David's questions, his need for resolve— these can't happen, since we haven't reached the last page.

In 1909, Henry Morrison, an American missionary, became ill after spending forty years serving in Africa. He and his wife packed their belongings to quietly board an ocean liner and return to New York. Two weeks later, the great ship was met by a large exuberant crowd to welcome one of the passengers who had been on safari, President Teddy Roosevelt. As the missionaries scanned the faces on the dock, they realized no one was there to welcome them home. Crestfallen, they lifted their bags and disembarked, checking into a cheap hotel. Henry went out to walk off his frustration, pouring out venom in prayer. He angrily contrasted their return with that of the president's—his was a holiday, theirs was a lifetime, and there was not a soul to meet them. A quiet voice from the heavens met his anguished rage: "You're not home yet."

There are three movements in David's song. In the first, he considers his situation (verses 1–4); in the second, his eyes are on his source of protection (verses 5–6); and finally, he searches for salvation for his people (verse 7).

David begins with what he sees around him, picking up the theme we first heard in Psalm 1—those who had no time for God lacked wisdom as they poured venom on those who passed by (Psalm 1:1). The rebels go further than the early description; they declare themselves free of the hindrance of a deity. And here in Psalm 14, he is less than polite; his words fire like shots from a gun. He calls those who say, "no God," fools.

With no one to answer, their greed is their guide—they mine people for power, they crush the weak to fulfill their cravings. He says that in turning aside from the peace of living under God's rule, their lives become chaotic.

Ethan was thrown out of home at age fifteen. His mum needed the room—his half sister's drug habit had her in a spin, and his brother moved back after he'd been found cheating again. Ethan needed to stay with a friend. Troubled and alone, he texted Mark. They'd known each other since the summer he'd wandered into a Bible club in the park. He'd met Mark's mum and remembered her stories of mountains shaking and rules written on stone by God—it was epic! He asked if he could stay at his place for a bit.

Mark's parents told their son the answer was yes, but that there were conditions: Ethan had to be in by curfew, let them know where he was, attend school every day, be at the house for meals, and call his mum once a week. And smoking and drugs weren't allowed in the house. Mark kicked the wall, scowling, annoyed. "But Dad, that's so harsh! He's not used to restrictions. Why stress him out with your stupid rules? He needs to feel that he's safe."

His mum's eyes sparkled. "Safety is exactly what he'll get! Look around, lovely boy. When you walk through that door, you know exactly what you'll find. The boundaries we place on our family have made our home settled and stable. Ethan carries turmoil in his body—he never knows what to expect, the rules keep changing." She pulled her son closer and said, "We live by a code from an ancient book that's filled with respect for the other. And quite honestly, Mark, it works."

The answer dazed him. He'd always thought their rules overbearing and never thought twice about the haven he enjoyed.

That night Ethan put his feet between crisp, cool sheets. The welcome of Mark's family had been puzzling; their instructions were a surprise. Despite the confusion of all the new ways, he kept his side of the pact. His teachers were baffled at the change in his grades, and back home, his mother's heart warmed from his weekly phone calls.

The ways of God may seem demanding, since they ask us to set aside our rights. They change the game from trying to be the most important to something altogether different. When the Ten Commandments were written by the finger of God, we were given a hint at another kingdom. A radical

idea was birthed into the world that altered our system of values. God gave laws that no one could stand over, ones that would govern kings. His rule gave women and children honor, gave slaves the same value as emperors. It placed every person on the same ground, measured all by the same scale. And then God freely invited people to walk into the covenant, to abide by its limits, shelter under its code. It let someone be bigger than them.[1]

The second part of David's song (verses 5–6) speaks of eternal protection and of the trust that its safety brings: this is a subject where David is an expert! He has known that no matter how fierce the battle, his eternal companion is stronger; that no matter how disorienting his insecurities, God will see through the fog.

David ends this lament with hope we would not have dreamed he possessed a few verses before. Despite the monstrous acts around them, David stands with the righteous and declares that they're safe. He sees the future filled with freedom and songs of joy, for "we're not home yet."

The fool has said in his heart,
"There is no God."
They are corrupt,
They have done abominable works,
There is none who does good.

PSALM 14, VERSE 1

This passage has boomed from loudspeakers for decades, condemning atheists as fools, dissenters as brainless. Have you heard it? It's uncomfortable; it feels abusive.

"The fool has said in his heart, 'There is no God.'" Is David shaming those searching for truth?

I've wrestled with these words and questioned the text. It provokes, offends, and, perplexingly, doesn't seem to fit with surrounding psalms. Disturbing. It took a whole day of discomfort to see who is "the fool." The second line was so big, I was blinded to the crucial word.

Heart.

The location of the oath is the heart. David writes about those who have driven goodness from their *moral* core; whose greed trumps the value of all around; who feed on injustice and punish the poor. They have chosen a path far from virtue[2] so he calls them "abominable," "doing no good."

Now the song makes sense. It fits with the melody he's scripted. And my soul can rest! In the explosive statement I missed who he was writing to. The mail was addressed to someone else.

THE FOOL HAS SAID IN HIS HEART THE FOOL HAS SAID IN HIS HEART THE FOOL HAS SAID IN HIS HEART THE FOOL HAS SAID

HAS SAID IN HIS HEART THE FOOL HAS SAID

THE FOOL HAS SAID IN HIS HEART THE FOOL THE FOOLD

THERE said in his heart NO GOD

From the sublime to the ridiculous

The LORD looks down from heaven upon the children
of men,
To see if there are any who understand, who seek God.
They have all turned aside,
They have together become corrupt;
There is none who does good,
No, not one.

PSALM 14, VERSES 2 AND 3

The psalmist takes things further, outlining the corruption: it's the gangster stuffing his pockets with twenties as he makes people pay for protection; the official evicting vulnerable tenants in exchange for promotion and power.

People are in anguish; they're calling for mercy, but those in control have crushed them in mud. The proud have united, consuming and craving, endorsing their greed, using people like things.

The ancient warrior lifts up his quill, these tyrants and bullies "together have become corrupt. There is no good in them." But far from getting away with their exploitation, every action has been clocked, each thought weighed. Heaven hasn't missed a thing.

So I drew the eyes of God, stretching out across the plains, seeing beneath their burly bravado.

They thought they were sublime, people to be worshiped! But He sees them as they are, crawling and corrupt.

Breaking bread

Have all the workers of iniquity no knowledge,
Who eat up my people as they eat bread,
And do not call on the LORD?

PSALM 14, VERSE 4

We invite folk for dinner to enjoy their company, to make plans, to connect, to have fun. The food we eat is background activity, setting the tone for laughter and conversation. Sure, show-stopping mains and dazzling desserts may raise a comment, but bread? It's consumed thoughtlessly, torn up for fuel, the invisible part of the meal.

God's people are described as devoured bread, torn up and unseen.

And a memory comes, unbidden into our minds. It is Sunday, and vicars and pastors gather people to remember that night and that bread. In a loft, it was broken, dripping with wine, while their friend said that, likewise, He'd be ripped apart. And that festival weekend, it happened. Christ's body was torn.

The devouring injustice of it.

HAVE ALL THE WORKERS OF INIQUITY NO KNOWLEDGE?

AND DO NOT CALL ON THE LORD?

Running scared

There they are in great fear,
For God is with the generation of the righteous.
You shame the counsel of the poor,
But the LORD is his refuge.

PSALM 14, VERSES 5 AND 6

There are consequences to tearing people apart, to consuming them like food. David writes that each person is known. Even those who feel disposable, who count themselves worthless.

In my mind is the image of the misfit and the bullies. They square up, advancing to maul and to shame. He braces himself to take the beating, but none comes. Instead, he hears their frantic gasps. They turn and run from his tiny frame. Baffled, he checks his muscles! It can't be these that brought the fear! And, mystified, he turns.

Standing behind him, smiling and enormous, is a giant![3] *So awesome.*

The poem repeats and strengthens in tone. They've bullied and shamed David, but with God in his corner, their own fear becomes dread. He is safe in the shelter of the Almighty.

Hooray!

THERE THEY ARE IN GREAT FEAR

For God is with the generation of the righteous for God is with

God is with

You shame the counsel of the poor You shame th

refuge

Chain splitter!

Oh, that the salvation of Israel would come out of Zion!
When the LORD brings back the captivity of His people,
Let Jacob rejoice and Israel be glad.

PSALM 14, VERSE 7

This song has moved from sorrow to hope, from places of gloom to dancing joy! Corruption and self-centered greed pervade, but here, David spreads out a new day.

They are not alone. God identifies Himself as walking with the helpless, knowing their concerns, seeing their plight.

These weak ones are His. And far from shrugging His reluctance, He smiles upon them, scooping up the righteous, giving them a future. He is their refuge, protection, and chain shatterer.

Let there be joy!

Oh that the salvation of Israel

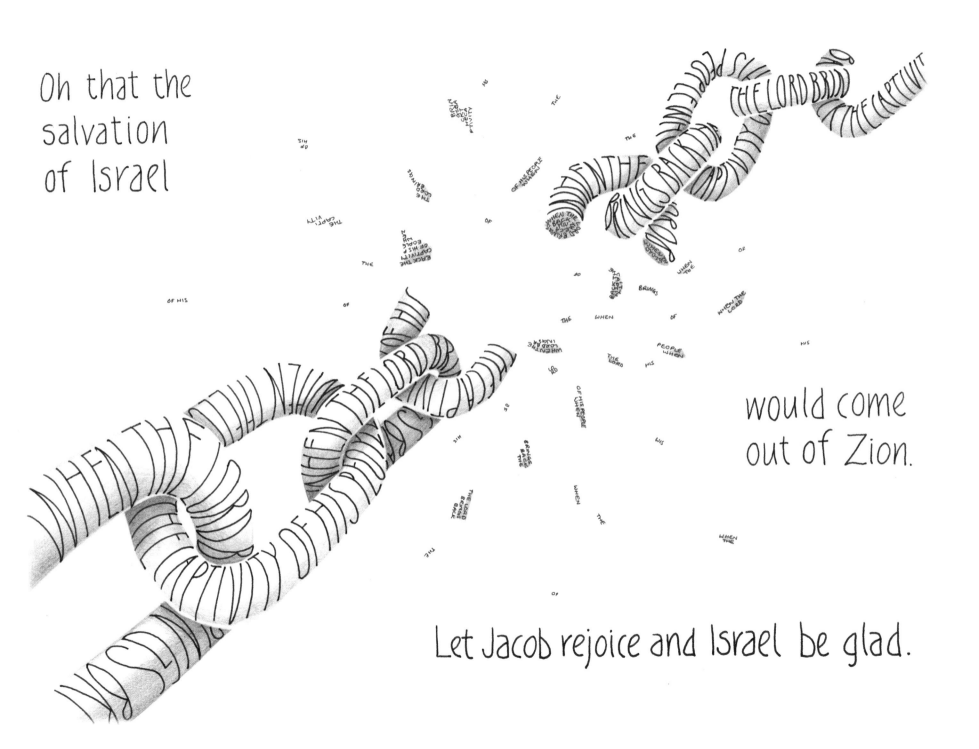

would come out of Zion.

Let Jacob rejoice and Israel be glad.

Conclusion

Through these pages we have moved into the landscape with the shepherd boy, now king. We have paced with him along the trail, heard his questions, his fears; watched his encounters with God and with evil, with the righteous and with his own heart.

David has surprised us, for despite profound unease in all the spaces of his life—physically as his enemies pursued him, mentally where self-doubt destabilized, spiritually where his sin seemed to thin out his soul—his stubborn trust in God has only steadily grown.

At times it feels like we're with him, standing on a cliff looking over the desert. He points out where battles were fought, where he hid, where he trembled, where he raged with God in despair. David doesn't deny his failures, nor belittle his fear. And what continues to astonish him is that God chose to be with him again and again.

God and the wicked, the righteous and himself—these are the characters of his songs. Let's spend a little time in their company.

God. David goes far beyond our Sunday school image of an eternal Being on a distant throne; of a wrath-filled deity throwing sulfur and then drowning the earth.

The Wicked. The psalmist shows us evil, through gripping details of atrocities up close. This ancient king doesn't stand aloof, sheltered by butlers and golden charms. David is a king who is there in the midst of it. He has seen those driven by malice, who hide and trap, oppress and abuse. His descriptions shimmer in their revelation of the acts of evil and of their source. His reaction to their malice throughout the text is telling. He is ready to defend the weak and calls on God to rise up; he stands up to protect the orphans, saying that the Lord is their great refuge. David has apprenticed himself to the God who is with us, Emmanuel (Matthew 1:23) in stark contrast to the evil that drives his foes.

The striking gap between the wicked and righteous, from the beginning to the end of the Psalter, is shame. They show neither remorse for wrongdoing nor humility for their offense; it makes for uncomfortable reading. We would understand if David got involved, to settle scores and put things right. But instead, with great trust, he steps back.

He asks the Almighty to judge. This hands-off approach perhaps stems from the way his Mentor deals with the wicked: the penalties for the wicked during their lives lie largely in their own hands. When they act with hatred, hatred's what they'll receive; when they oppress, they can expect the same back. And in eternity, their choice to be distant from God will be fulfilled for them forever. They'll be separated from His company and home in death, just as they chose in their life. It's a monumental plan, fair in its reach, devastating in its finality.

The Righteous. Those who follow God through life do not walk on petaled pathways. We read of them riddled by depletion and pain, attracting the contempt of the strong. This is no sales pitch of comfort or luxury. So, what is the draw? What makes them pursue a creed and an Almighty who was equally maligned? There are things far greater than wealth or adulation; there is a peace in the soul that surpasses all charms. The righteous we meet in these pages of David's have souls that are unbounded by chains. They rise in worship; they sing in splendor; they walk a road with an eternal Friend and know their future will find them in His glory.

David. It is David's understanding of himself that shows some of the greatest insights in these fourteen psalms.

He has not painted a portrait of power, nor airbrushed a glowing band around his brow. The prize for him is not to be lauded as a monarch, blazing with strength and commanding legions, nor is it to appear adorned with halo, dazzling the world with wisdom. David is real. He meets the Almighty in the middle of his mess, bringing doubts and insecurities before the Ancient of Days. He doesn't clean up before he approaches the King. He arrives dirty—stained by his choices, bruised by the disdain of those he holds dear. In humility he asks God to clean him and heal him, both outside and within.

And we trace the outline of the young shepherd boy tasked with protecting sheep, brought in from the fields and anointed, surprised he has been chosen for greatness (1 Samuel 16:1–13).

We have met these four characters through each of David's songs, made discoveries, connected with sorrows and joy. And in tomorrow's chapter, we each will encounter the same: God, evil, the righteous, and ourselves.

What song shall we sing with the One who walks by our side?

Acknowledgments

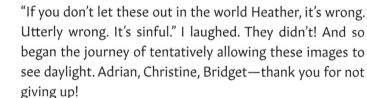

"If you don't let these out in the world Heather, it's wrong. Utterly wrong. It's sinful." I laughed. They didn't! And so began the journey of tentatively allowing these images to see daylight. Adrian, Christine, Bridget—thank you for not giving up!

Mrs. G. and Bible Stories Alive—for beginning my love of the Bible, through stories on a wind-up cassette recorder in Africa; for captivating my heart with your enormous God.

The Author of all—for writing me into Your story and filling my days with wonder.

Adrian—for decades of friendship and love; for three long years of caring for me when I couldn't stand for long enough to peel an egg (new health diagnostic!); for the joy of being by your side in this adventure of following God; for showing me that He is kind; for being like Him.

Julius Wong Loi Sing—inspirational professor, valued friend, who opened the book of Psalms and transported our class to the gates of heaven.

Colin—for writing stunning theology into transcendent music of praise and lament; for blazing a trail of courageous creativity.

John Ellis—for your beautiful reflections that became the title of this book.

Amy Simpson, Sara Gordon, Andrew and Brenda Marin, Norma, Nicola, Steve and Liz—for believing in what I couldn't see; for showing me this was worth doing.

Amanda Cleary Eastep—for your encouraging attention to every edit and for joy through the process.

Trillia Newbell and the Moody Publishers editing team—for making this endeavor about God and about people.

Balgove Larder—for wonderful staff who brought morning coffee and scrambled eggs to my busy writing table. Thank you for giving me the corner booth!

St. Andrews Swimmers—for fabulous chats in the freezing water, stirring energy, joy, and urging me on.

My deep affection and thanks to many precious family and friends—for joy, kindness, and companionship on this adventure.

Notes

INTRODUCTION

1. Athanasius (AD 296–373), "Treatise on the Psalms," as quoted in Michael Bushell, *The Songs of Zion* (Pittsburgh: Crown and Covenant Publications, 1980), 94.

2. Anselm of Canterbury (c. 1033–1109), quoted in Colin E. Gunton, *Revelation and Reason: Prolegomena to Systematic Theology*, ed. P. H. Brazier (London: T&T Clark, 2008), 131.

3. Julius Wong Loi Sing, "Applying the Psalms in the Christian Life," in Herbert W. Bateman and D. Brent Sandy, *Interpreting the Psalms for Teaching and Preaching* (St. Louis: Chalice Press, 2010), 206–18.

4. Ibid.

5. Eugene Peterson, "1 Peter 5:7," *The Message Bible* (Colorado Springs: NavPress, 2004).

6. Irenaeus of Lyons (AD 130–202), "Irenaeus against Heresies," in *The Apostolic Fathers with Justin Martyr and Irenaeus*, ed. Alexander Roberts et al., vol. 1 (Buffalo: Christian Literature Publishing Company, 1885), 490.

7. John Coe, "Lesson 1: Resisting the Temptation of Moral Formation (Part 1)," BiblicalTraining.org, https://www.biblicaltraining.org/library/resisting-temptation-moral-formation-i/spiritual-formation/john-coe.

8. Ibid.

9. Jewish prayer Modeh Ani, *Encyclopaedia Judaica*, 2nd ed. (Detroit: Macmillan, 2007), 14:406.

10. C. S. Lewis, *Letters to Malcolm: Chiefly on Prayer* (London: William Collins, 2020).

11. Richard H. Schmidt, *God Seekers: Twenty Centuries of Christian Spiritualities* (Grand Rapids: Wm. B. Eerdmans, 2008), 74.

12. *NIV Study Bible: New International Version* (Grand Rapids: Zondervan, 2011), 1048. Used by permission.

13. Though widely attributed to Athanasius, these words are a summary, not a direct quote. See Bernhard W. Anderson, *Out of the Depths: The Psalms Speak for Us Today*, 3rd ed. (Louisville: Westminster John Knox Press, 2000), ix. Citing the "Letter to Marcellinus on the Interpretation of the Psalms," Anderson writes, "most of Scripture speaks to us while the Psalms speak for us."

14. Psalm 56:8; Isaiah 55:12; Isaiah 40:31.

PSALM 1

1. John Goldingay, *Psalms: Psalms 1–41*, vol. 1 (Ada, MI: Baker Academic, 2007), 23.

2. Ibid., 58.

3. Exodus 19 and 20.

4. Ralph Waldo Emerson, "Self-Reliance and Other Essays" (Mineola, NY: Dover Thrift Editions: Philosophy), 25.

PSALM 2

1. Stephen Charnock and James McCosh, *The Complete Works of Stephen Charnock*, vol. 1 (Edinburgh: James Nichol, 1864), 279. Revised into contemporary English from the 1600s.

2. C. H. Spurgeon, *Praying Successfully* (New Kensington, PA: Whitaker House, 1997), 23.

PSALM 3

1. 2 Samuel 13:20.

PSALM 4

1. Psalm 4:2.

2. William Roscoe Thayer, *The Life and Letters of John Hay* (Boston: Houghton Mifflin, 1915), 82.

PSALM 5

1. A. W. Tozer, *The Knowledge of the Holy: The Attributes of God: Their Meaning in the Christian Life* (New York: Harper & Row, 1961), 9.

2. Author paraphrase of Psalm 5:4–6.

3. Walter Brueggemann, *The Message of the Psalms: A Theological Commentary* (Minneapolis: Augsburg Publishing House, 1984), 77.

4. Erwin Raphael McManus, *Way of the Warrior: An Ancient Path to Inner Peace* (Colorado Springs: WaterBrook, 2021), 1.

PSALM 6

1. Saint Augustine, "Prayer of Saint Augustine," Augustinian Spirituality, June 29, 2020, https://augustinianspirituality.org/2020/06/29/prayer-of-saint-augustine/.

2. John Calvin, quoted in David G. Benner, *The Gift of Being Yourself: The Sacred Call to Self-Discovery*, expanded ed. (Downers Grove, IL: IVP, 2015), 22.

3. Charlie Mackesy, *Boy, the Mole, the Fox and the Horse* (San Francisco: HarperOne, 2021), n.p.

4. C. H. Spurgeon, *The Treasury of David*, vol. 1 (New York: Marshall Brothers Limited, 1869), 58.

PSALM 7

1. Agatha Christie, *Miss Marple: The Complete Short Stories* (New York: HarperCollins, 2011), 8.

2. W. Graham Scroggie, *The Psalter Volume I Psalms 1 to 41* (London: Marshall, Morgan and Scott, 1931), 23.

3. Charles Wesley, first published in 1739 in "Hymns and Sacred Poems." "And can it be that I should gain," *Complete Mission Praise* compiled by P. Horrobin and Greg Levers (London: Harper Collins, 2005), 33.

4. Full disclosure: There is a mistake in this image. I made it after drawing for three or four hours. I was going to begin all over again, but thought, as it's speaking about debris and ditches, it should remain in its imperfection.

PSALM 8

1. C. S. Lewis, *Reflections on the Psalms* (New York: Harcourt, Brace and Company, 1958), 132.

2. Richard Exley, et al. *Dangers, Toils & Snares: Resisting the Hidden Temptations of Ministry* (Portland: Multnomah Books, 1994), 102.

3. Augustine of Hippo, and R. P. H. Green, *On Christian Teaching* (Oxford: Oxford University Press, 2008), Book 1.27–28.
Augustine, *Concerning the City of God Against the Pagans* (New York: Penguin Books, 2003), Book 15, Section 22.

4. Ralph Waldo Emerson, "Self-Reliance and Other Essays" (Mineola, NY: Dover Thrift Editions: Philosophy), 25.

5. Matthew 3:13–17.

6. James E. Smith, *The Wisdom Literature and Psalms* (Joplin, MO: College Press Pub. Co., 1996), 223.

7. Psalm 8:4 (ESV).

PSALM 9

1. Paraphrase of Psalm 9:1–3.

2. George MacDonald, *The Last Castle*, ed. Dan Hamilton (Wheaton, IL: Victor Books, 1986), 172.

3. T. S. Eliot, *Complete Poems and Plays: 1909–1950* (New York: Harcourt Brace and Company, 1952), 119.

4. Charles Price for the Standing Liturgical Commission, *Introducing the Proposed Book of Common Prayer*, 1689 (New York: Seabury Press, 1977).

PSALM 10

1. The picture began life as small words, sighing across a room. As the meditation on David's circumstance deepened, the whisper widened to a roar across space. It passed through Saturn's rings—a microbe to the Mighty!

PSALM 11

1. "Pride & Prejudice" (film), directed by Joe Wright (2005), based on the novel by Jane Austen.

2. Craig A. Blaising, Carmen S. Hardin, Thomas C. Oden, *Psalms 1–50* (Westmont, IL: InterVarsity Press, 2014), 95.

3. The Black Eyed Peas, "Where Is the Love?" (track 1), *Elephunk*, will.i.am Music Group, 2003.

4. A word on the perfect church—I switched my culturally flawed glasses and saw through the shiny beauty! We found people who were real and precious and dear. People who changed our lives!

5. "Sleepy Hollow" (film), directed by Tim Burton, 1999, based on "The Legend of Sleepy Hollow" by Washington Irving.

PSALM 12

1. John M. Perkins, *One Blood: Parting Words to the Church on Race and Love* (Chicago: Moody, 2018), 66.

2. William Shakespeare, *Hamlet*, Act III, Scene I.

3. Psalm 12:5.

4. Kevin Charles Belmonte, *Defiant Joy: The Remarkable Life & Impact of G. K. Chesterton* (Nashville: Thomas Nelson, 2011), 288.

PSALM 13

1. *The Poems of Dylan Thomas*, ed. J. Goodby (London: Weidenfeld and Nicolson, 2014, 2016), 193.

PSALM 14

1. Further writing on this from Jonathan Sacks, *Covenant and Conversation: Exodus: The Book of Redemption* (New Milford, CT: Maggid Books, 2010), 149ff.

2. Francis Brown et al., *Enhanced Brown-Driver-Briggs Hebrew and English Lexicon* (Oxford: Clarendon Press, 1977), 524.

3. The inspiration for this story comes from the following children's book: Julia Donaldson and Axel Scheffler, *The Gruffalo* (London: Macmillan Children's Books, 2015).